D1751719

Armin Lindauer
**Die Berliner Mauer –
Der Anfang vom Ende**
*The Berlin Wall –
The Beginning of the End*

Die Teilung Berlins
Division of Berlin
F Französische Zone *French Sector*
UDSSR Sowjetische Zone *Sowjet Sector*
USA Amerikanische Zone *American Sector*
GB Britische Zone *British Sector*

Grenzübergänge
Border crossings
1. Bornholmer Straße
2. Chausseestraße
3. Invalidenstraße
4. Friedrichstraße
5. Checkpoint Charlie
6. Heinrich-Heine-Straße
7. Oberbaumbrücke
8. Sonnenallee
9. Dreilinden/Wannsee
10. Heerstraße/Staaken
11. Heiligensee/Stolpe

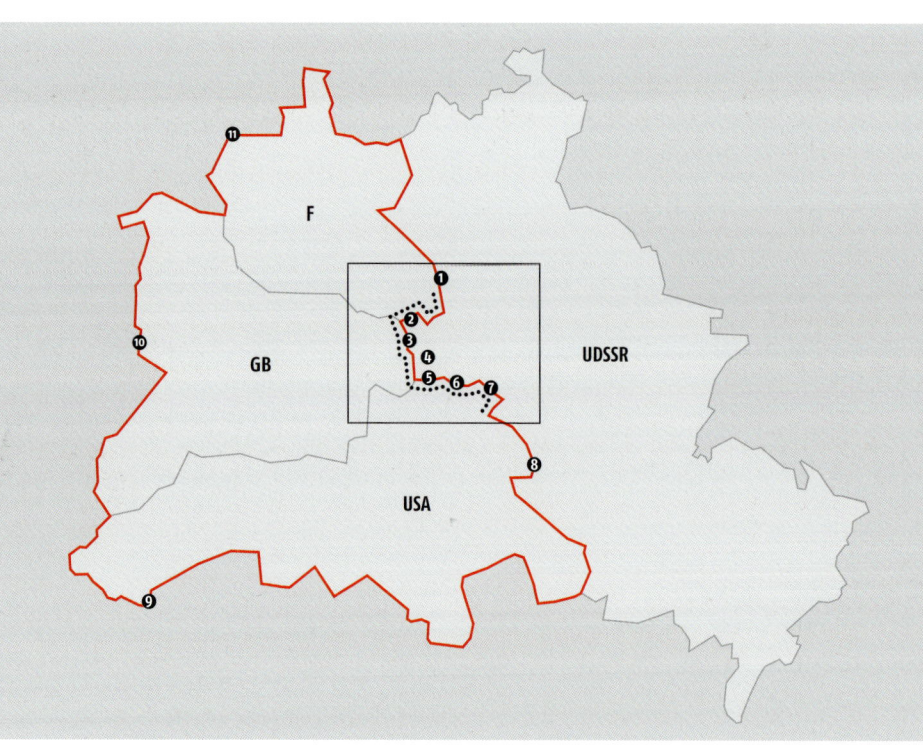

— Verlauf der Berliner Mauer
Course of the Berlin Wall

···· Entlang dieser Strecke entstanden die Fotografien
The photos were taken along this part of the course

— Besetzte Zonen
Sectors

☐ Detailansicht Karte Seite 94
Details map page 94

Gesamtlänge 155 km
Total length 155 km

Höhe 3,8 bis 4,1 m
Height 3.8 to 4.1 m

Armin Lindauer
Die Berliner Mauer –
Der Anfang vom Ende
The Berlin Wall –
The Beginning of the End
Mit einem Text von
Text written by
Andreas Schenk

EDITION**PANORAMA**

1984–86

14|15 26|27 38|39 50|51
16|17 28|29 40|41 52|53
18|19 30|31 42|43 54|55
20|21 32|33 44|45 56|57
22|23 34|35 46|47 58|59
24|25 36|37 48|49 60|61

Inhalt *Content*

1991

2007

62|63

64|65

66|67

68|69

70|71

72|73

74|75

1999

76|77

78|79

80|81

82|83

84|85

86|87

88|89

90|91

	2	Karte: Die Teilung Berlins *Map: Division of Berlin*
	6	Vorwort *Preface*
	8	Die Berliner Mauer *The Berlin Wall*
1984–86	14	Bernauer Straße
	19	Ebertstraße
	20	Stresemannstraße
	22	Niederkirchnerstraße
	34	Zimmerstraße
	37	Axel-Springer-Straße
	40	Sebastianstraße
	42	Luckauer Straße, Waldemarstraße
	48	Bethaniendamm
	67	Lohmühlenstraße
1991	70	Potsdamer Platz
1999	76	Mühlenstraße, East Side Gallery
2007	80	Bernauer Straße
	92	Karte: Die Teilung Berlins (Ausschnitt) *Map: Division of Berlin (Detail)*
	93	Index *Index*
	94	Die Grenzsicherungsanlage *Border security installation*
	95	Biografie *Biography*
	96	Impressum *Imprint*

**Die Berliner Mauer – Der Anfang vom Ende
Armin Lindauer** ■ Anfang der achtziger Jahre ziehe ich nach West-Berlin. Es ist die Zeit des Kalten Krieges, 1979 wird der NATO-Doppelbeschluss gefasst und 1983 wird mit der daraus resultierenden Nachrüstung begonnen. Die USA stationieren Pershing-II-Raketen (Seite 66) und Marschflugkörper, sogenannte Cruise Missiles, in der BRD. ■ Seit 1975 wird die Berliner Mauer wieder umgebaut. Es ist der vierte Umbau und wird bis zu ihrem Fall im Jahre 1989 der letzte bleiben. Die schmalen, waagerechten Betonplatten werden durch breite, senkrechte ersetzt, die fugenlos miteinander verbunden sind. Erst diese Veränderung wird eine komplette Bemalung ermöglichen. ■ Ende der siebziger Jahre kann von einer Graffiti-Szene, von einer Graffiti-Kultur oder -Bewegung noch nicht die Rede sein. Das ändert sich zu Beginn der Achtziger. Einzelne Vorläufer wie Gérard Zlotykamien, der seit den sechziger Jahren in Paris tätig ist und Harald Naegeli, der Ende der Siebziger als „der Sprayer von Zürich" bekannt wird, müssen als Anreger und Wegbereiter gesehen werden. Naegeli wird schließlich angeklagt und zu einer Gefängnisstrafe verurteilt. Im Westen wird das Bemalen von Bauwerken als Sachbeschädigung mit empfindlichen Strafen geahndet. ■ Als Graffitimaler beginnen, die Berliner Mauer für sich zu entdecken, kann man nicht wissen, wie die DDR darauf reagieren wird. Schließlich gehört die Mauer einschließlich eines Laufstreifens von wenigen Metern Breite auf der Westseite zu ihrem Staatsgebiet. Immer wieder kommen Grenzer durch Türen in der Mauer, sogenannte Schlupftore (Seite 19) oder durch die Grenzübergänge, um auf der Westseite zu patrouillieren. Die Westmächte sehen dem Treiben der Mauermaler meist tatenlos zu und scheinen kein besonderes Interesse daran zu haben, die Graffiti zu verhindern. Im Gegenteil, man möchte vermuten, dass ihnen die dort niedergeschriebene Kritik, sofern sie gegen den Osten gerichtet ist, gerade recht kommt. Da die Bemalung von den Grenzsoldaten kaum zu verhindern ist und der Westen keine Amtshilfe leistet, entsteht ein Freiraum, der, sobald er erkannt ist, ausgiebig genutzt wird. Zunächst sind es knappe Parolen oder einfache Bemalungen, die schnell gemacht sind (Seite 58). Später werden sie zunehmend komplexer und ausgearbeiteter (Seite 45). ■ Zu Beginn der achtziger Jahre entsteht in Berlin eine neue Kunstrichtung, die unter dem Begriff „Neue Wilde" für Aufsehen sorgt und weltweiten Erfolg hat. Ihr Stil hat expressive, gegenständliche, stark farbige und mit Graffiti-Elementen versehene Züge. In ihren Bildern wird die Mauer als Motiv und Thema immer wieder aufgegriffen. Auch bei einer Reihe von Mauerbemalungen lassen sich stilistische Anleihen aus diesem Umfeld feststellen. Viele der „Neuen Wilden" und einige der Mauermaler studieren an der Hochschule der Künste Berlin. Vermutlich kennt man sich oder weiß zumindest voneinander. Als weiterer Anreger und stilistisches Vorbild gilt mit seinen Strichmännchen der aus dem Osten stammende Künstler A. R. Penck. So entstehen aus den unterschiedlichsten Quellen subversive und überaus vielfältige Bemalungen. ■ Die politische Dimension der Bemalung ergibt sich schon aus dem Ort, an dem sie stattfindet. Sie kritisiert und demaskiert beide Seiten. Die Mauer, das Symbol der Teilung, wird jetzt auch zum Symbol des Widerstandes, sie wird ein sich veränderndes Spiegelbild des Zeitgeistes. Ihre Bemalung ist und bleibt Momentaufnahme, da sie immer wieder neu übermalt wird. Einige Parolen, die mir gut in Erinnerung geblieben und nicht von mir dokumentiert sind, lauten: „Steter Tropfen höhlt den Stein – Bitte hier pinkeln"; „Next Coke 10.000 km"; „Being against the wall is like fucking for virginity"; „Mauern gilt nicht"; „Let my Paint die with the Wall". So wie die Graffiti vielleicht dazu beiträgt, die Mauer zu Fall zu bringen, so hat das Verschwinden der Mauer die Graffiti beseitigt. ■ Von Beginn an bin ich von der Fülle der Stile, der Experimentierfreude, den persönlichen und politischen Anliegen, Mitteilungen und Parolen angezogen und fasziniert. Also beginne ich auf Exkursionen entlang der Mauer diese Mitteilungen zu dokumentieren. Zunächst ausschnitthaft, später zunehmend auch längere Abschnitte. Das Konzept ist, keine wechselnden Perspektiven zu wählen, sondern die Bemalungen sachlich frontal zu zeigen. Dazu wird immer auch ein Stück Boden vor der Mauer und ein Stück Himmel mit Gebäuden oder Wachtürmen gezeigt. Durch diese Verortung der Graffiti auf der Mauer und ihrer Umgebung werden auch Bemalungen von lediglich persönlichen Mitteilungen zu politischen Statements. Mauer und Bemalung sind untrennbar miteinander verbunden und steigern gegenseitig ihre Wirkung und Bedeutung. ■ Spätere Graffiti, wie die nach dem Mauerfall bemalten Reststücke am Potsdamer Platz (Seite 70 bis 75) oder die East Side Gallery (Seite 76 bis 79), haben ihre politische Brisanz verloren und sind lediglich dekorative Nostalgie-, Foto- oder Sammelobjekte. Der Verlust der politischen Qualität scheint sich auch auf die künstlerische Qualität der nach dem Mauerfall entstandenen Graffiti auszuwirken. ■ Am 9. November 1989 ist die Mauer offen, plötzlich und unerwartet, „ab sofort" wie auf allen Sendern zu hören ist. Wie viele andere fahre ich zum nächstliegenden Grenzübergang, der Invalidenstraße, um mir ein Bild davon zu machen. Meine Fotoexkursionen habe ich vergessen, sie liegen Jahre zurück und man kann noch nicht ahnen, dass die Mauer nun innerhalb kurzer Zeit verschwinden wird. Erst viel später wird mir die geschichtliche Bedeutung dieser Aufnahmen bewusst. Intensive Recherchen haben ergeben, dass es keine vergleichbare Reihe an Fotografien gibt. In diesem Buch wird nun zum ersten Mal ein großer Teil dieser Sammlung gezeigt. ■ Allen, die am Gelingen des Buches beteiligt waren, möchte ich sehr herzlich danken. Dank an meine Verleger Bernhard und Sebastian Wipfler, die dieses Projekt gewagt und engagiert begleitet haben. Dank an Heike van Laak, die mir damals ihren VW-Käfer für die Exkursionen geliehen und an Nadine Schreiner, die mir bei den unterschiedlichsten Recherchen geholfen hat. Dank auch an die Fachleute von Electronic Publishing Service und an Bianca Radke, die meine wiederholten Korrekturen ertragen haben. Ohne all diese Unterstützung hätte dieses Projekt nicht realisiert werden können.

The Berlin Wall – The Beginning of the End
Armin Lindauer ■ At the beginning of the 1980s, I moved to West Berlin. It was the era of the Cold War, in 1979 the NATO Double-Track Decision was made and the resulting rearmament began in 1983. The USA stationed Pershing 2 tactical missiles (page 66) and so-called cruise missiles in the Federal Republic of Germany.
■ The Berlin Wall was being renovated since 1975, the fourth renovation was to be the last until its final fall in 1989. The narrow horizontal concrete slabs were replaced by wide vertical slabs seamlessly joined together. It was this change which would enable the Wall to be painted from end-to-end. ■ By the end of the 1970s, there still wasn't a so-called graffiti scene, graffiti culture or movement. However, this changed at the beginning of the 1980s. Individual pioneers such as Gérard Zlotykamien, who had been working in Paris since the 1960s and Harald Naegeli, who became known by the end of the 1970s as "the sprayer of Zurich", must be regarded as the initiators and groundbreakers. Naegeli was finally prosecuted and sentenced to a term of imprisonment as the West punished any defacing of buildings as damage to property which incurred major fines.
■ When the graffiti artists began to discover the Berlin Wall as a canvas for their self-expression it was impossible to gauge how the GDR would react. After all, the Wall and the strip of land a few metres wide on the Western side was part of its territory. Again and again, border guards appeared through doors in the wall, so-called side entrances (page 19) or via the border crossing-points, in order to patrol on the West side. The Western powers generally regarded the actions of the wall artists with equanimity, and seemed to have no particular interest in putting a stop to activities. On the contrary, one might suspect that the criticism expressed here suited them down to the ground, provided that it was directed at the East. Since the painting of the Wall could not be prevented by the border guards, and the West provided no official assistance in the matter, freedom of action developed, and any empty space discovered was quickly used to the full. At first, only mere words or simple paintings which could be applied quickly appeared (page 58). Later they became increasingly more complex and sophisticated (page 45). ■ At the beginning of the 1980s, a new art genre developed in Berlin, attracting great attention and enjoying worldwide acclaim under the name of the "Neue Wilde". Its style comprised expressive, objective features characterised by strong-coloured components and graffiti elements. Its imagery repeatedly took up the Wall as a motif and a theme. A series of wall paintings also demonstrated stylistic links with this setting. Many of the "Neue Wilde" and some of the wall-painters studied at the Berlin School of Art. They probably knew each other, or at least had heard of each other. Another stimulant and stylistic model was artist A.R. Penck, originally from the East, with his matchstick men. In this way, subversive and extremely varied wall paintings developed from a great variety of sources.
■ The political dimension of the painting stemmed from the place at which it was performed. It criticised and unmasked both sides. The Wall, the symbol of division, now also became a symbol of resistance, becoming a varying reflection of the spirit of the times. Its painting was and remains a snapshot of the moment, since the canvas was repainted time and time again. Some of the sayings which have stuck in my memory which I have not previously documented include: "Constant dripping wears the stone – Please pee here"; "Next Coke 10,000 km"; "Being against the wall is like fucking for virginity"; "Walls don't work"; "Let my paint die with the Wall". Just as the graffiti perhaps contributed to bringing down the Wall, it also appropriately disappeared with it. ■
From the outset, I was attracted and fascinated by the wealth of different styles, the joy of experimentation, the personal and political subjects, messages and words. I therefore started to document these messages during the course of excursions along the Wall. Initially only as excerpts, but later in increasingly longer sections. The concept was not to choose any alternating perspectives, but to show the paintings objectively from a frontal standpoint, always showing a little of the ground in front of the wall and some of the skyline above featuring buildings or watchtowers. Through this localisation of the graffiti on the Wall and its surrounding area, the representation of purely personal messages turns into a political statement. The Wall and its painting become inseparably joined, mutually emphasising each other's effect and significance. ■ Later graffiti, such as the remains of the Wall on the Potsdamer Platz (page 70 to 75) painted after its fall or the East Side Gallery (page 76 to 79), have lost their political import, and are nothing more than decorative nostalgia, mere subjects for photos or collectors items. The loss of the political significance also seems to have had an effect on the artistic quality of the graffiti applied after the demolition of the Wall. ■
On 9 November 1989, suddenly and unexpectedly, the Wall is re-opened, "with immediate effect", as can be heard on every radio station. Like many others, I drove to the nearest border crossing point, the Invalidenstraße, to see for myself what was going on. My photo excursions were a long time ago and are forgotten, and it is almost impossible to believe that the Wall will now soon disappear. Only much later do I become aware of the historical importance of these photographs. Exhaustive research has shown that no other comparable series of photographs exists. A large part of this collection is now being published for the first time in this book. ■ I would like to express my sincere thanks to all those involved in the success of this book. My thanks go out to my publishers Bernhard and Sebastian Wipfler, who accepted and enthusiastically supervised this project, to Heike van Laak, who lent me her VW Beetle at the time for my excursions, and to Nadine Schreiner, who assisted me in the extensive research required. I also would like to thank the experts at EPS and Bianca Radke, who endured my repeated corrections. Without all this support, this project would not have been possible.

Die Berliner Mauer: Hier lacht der Bär
Andreas Schenk ■ Ob die Fotografien dieses Bildbandes die Vorder- oder Rückseite der Mauer zeigen, ist, wie so vieles, eine Frage des Standpunktes. Von Westberlin aus gesehen, war es die Vorderseite – die Seite, die im Unterschied zur anderen gefahrlos fotografiert werden konnte und die, obwohl sie zu einer scharf bewachten Grenzanlage gehörte, auf weiten Strecken auch Kunstobjekt wurde, bemalt und besprüht mit illegalen Graffiti. Zwischen den zahlreichen Bildern standen auch Worte und Sätze – Mitteilungen, Parolen und Statements. Eine der vielen Aufschriften lautete: „Hier lacht der Bähr", wie auf einem der Fotos zu lesen ist. Wer immer dies geschrieben hat, meinte wohl trotz des orthographischen Fehlers, das Wappentier Berlins, der damals geteilten Stadt, in der es denn auch zwei Bären gab, einen im Westberliner und einen im Ostberliner Wappen. Auf welchen der beiden Bären sich der Spruch bezog oder ob hier die Einheit der Stadt vorausgesetzt war, bleibt im Unklaren. Zum Lachen aber gab es an diesem Ort, dem Symbol der Unfreiheit und der Spaltung Deutschlands, eigentlich keinen Anlass. ■ Nach dem Ende des Zweiten Weltkriegs war Berlin in den Sog des Machtkampfes zwischen der Sowjetunion und den Westalliierten USA, Großbritannien und Frankreich geraten, so dass sich die Demarkationslinie zwischen der sowjetischen Besatzungszone und den Westzonen zur innerstädtischen Grenze entwickelte. Wie verhärtet die Front war, zeigte die Berliner Blockade von 1948/49, mit der die Sowjetunion die Bevölkerung Westberlins von der Lebensmittelversorgung abschnitt – ein Akt der Erpressung, gegen den die „Rosinenbomber" der amerikanischen und britischen Armee erfolgreich anflogen. Die Gründung der BRD im September 1949 und die der DDR im Oktober desselben Jahres zementierten die Teilung. Fortan lebten die Westberliner auf einer – mehr oder weniger – bundesrepublikanisch geprägten Insel inmitten der DDR, während die Ostberliner wieder Hauptstadtbewohner waren. ■ Dass Ostberlin aufgrund des Besatzungsstatus kein integraler Bestandteil der DDR war, scherte die Führungskader der Republik wenig. Auch dass sich ihr Staat demokratisch nannte ohne dies zu sein, kümmerte sie nicht. Die SED ließ viele Wahrheiten nicht gelten, obwohl sie von sich das hohe Lied der Unfehlbarkeit sang. Die Hymne „Die Partei, die Partei, die hat immer recht" erklang zum ersten Mal 1950 und wurde danach noch unzählige Male angestimmt, so als wollten sich die Machthaber immer wieder selbst versichern, dass ihr Weg der richtige sei. Das Gegenteil bewies die „Abstimmung mit den Füßen". Bis zum Jahr des Mauerbaus 1961 flohen 2,6 Millionen Menschen in die Bundesrepublik, was dem „Arbeiter- und Bauernstaat" neben dem ideologischen Schaden auch volkswirtschaftliche Probleme infolge des Verlustes von Arbeitskräften bereitete. Die DDR-Führung versuchte zwar der Abwanderung entgegen zu wirken, indem sie die innerdeutsche Grenze ab 1952 durch Sperrzonen, Zäune und Wachposten abriegelte. Dies führte aber nur dazu, dass sich die Fluchtwege im zweigeteilten Berlin bündelten. Auch Bürger anderer Ostblockstaaten setzten sich über die innerstädtische Demarkationslinie in den Westen ab. ■ Die Staatssicherheit hatte wohl schon lange mit dem Gedanken gespielt, die „Schlupflöcher" inmitten Berlins mit einer Mauer zu schließen. Die Planung erfolgte unter dem Siegel der Verschwiegenheit, was der Erste Sekretär des Zentralkomitees der SED, Walter Ulbricht, wohl einen Moment etwas zu genau nahm. Denn am 15. Juni 1961 versicherte er „Niemand hat die Absicht eine Mauer zu errichten", obwohl noch niemand öffentlich von einem solchen Grenzbauwerk gesprochen hatte. Mancher dürfte sich darauf seinen Reim gemacht haben. ■ Und so flohen in den ersten beiden Augustwochen des Jahres 1961 über 47 000 Menschen. Gerade noch rechtzeitig, denn in der Nacht vom 12. auf dem 13. August 1961 rückten die Einheiten der Nationalen Volksarmee, der Grenz- und der Volkspolizei sowie Angehörige der Betriebskampftruppen an, um die Sektorengrenze nach Westberlin abzusperren. Zwei Tage später, am 15. August, machten sich die Bauarbeiter ans Werk, während westliche Nachrichtensender im freien Teil Berlins Stellung bezogen. Kamerateams und Fotografen hielten dramatische Szenen fest: etwa die Flucht eines Volksarmisten, der sich mit einem Satz über den Stacheldraht in die Freiheit rettete. Oder die Frau, die aus dem Fenster eines an der Grenze stehenden Hauses kletterte. Zwei Männer versuchten sie zurückzuziehen, dann gaben sie auf. Unten wartete die Westberliner Feuerwehr mit einem Sprungtuch. Diese Bilder waren im DDR-Fernsehen freilich nicht zu sehen. Dort flimmerte anderes, erbaulicheres über den Äther, etwa die beliebte Unterhaltungssendung „Da lacht der Bär", die bis 1965 einmal im Monat aus dem Ostberliner Friedrichstadtpalast ausgestrahlt wurde. Vor dem Mauerbau warben die Moderatoren für ein geeintes Deutschland. Danach vermieden sie dieses Thema. Ob der Spruch vom lachenden Bären auf den Titel dieser Sendung anspielte? ■ Die DDR-Führung mauerte Westberlin ein, um die eigene Bevölkerung einzusperren. Ausbruchsversuche endeten häufig tödlich. Am 24. August 1961 fielen die ersten Schüsse. Sie trafen den 24-jährigen Günther Litfin, als er den Berlin-Spandauer Schifffahrtskanal nach Westberlin durchschwimmen wollte. Für die Hinterbliebenen der Opfer musste es sich wie Hohn anhören, dass die SED die Mauer zum „antifaschistischen Schutzwall" erklärte. Doch der Freiheitswille ließ sich nicht brechen. Einige Flüchtlinge entkamen auf spektakuläre Weise, indem sie Tunnel unter der Mauer hindurch gruben oder mit selbst gebastelten Fluggeräten über die Grenze flogen. Andere wagten den direkten Weg durch die Grenzanlage, die allerdings so perfide geplant war, dass sie oft zur tödlichen Falle wurde. ■ Über weite Strecken verliefen zwei parallel geführte Mauern, eine in wenigen Metern Entfernung von der Demarkationslinie, die andere als Abgrenzung zu den Wohngebieten, Straßen und Plätzen Ostberlins. Im Geländestreifen dazwischen standen neben Zäunen aus Stachel-

The Berlin Wall: Here laughs the bear
Andreas Schenk ■ Whether the photographs of this illustrated volume show the front or rear side of the Wall is, like so many other things, a question of the standpoint. Seen from West Berlin, it was the front side – the side which in contrast to the other could be photographed without danger, and which, although it was a closely guarded border, also became an art object for much of its length, painted and sprayed with illegal graffiti. Amongst the numerous pictures were also words and sentences – messages, sayings and statements. One of the many inscriptions ran: "Here laughs the bear", as can be seen on one of the photos. Whoever wrote this most probably meant the heraldic animal of Berlin, the city which was divided at the time, and in which there were therefore two bears, one on the West Berlin coat of arms and one on that of East Berlin. To which of the two bears the words refer is unclear; perhaps it even presupposed the reunification of the city. There was really no occasion to laugh at this place, the symbol of the bondage and division of Germany. ■ Following the end of the Second World War, Berlin was caught up in the power struggle between the Soviet Union and the western allies of the USA, Great Britain and France, so that the demarcation line between the Soviet occupation zone and the western zones developed into an inner-city border. How tense the situation was then was demonstrated by the Berlin Blockade of 1948/49, by which the Soviet Union cut off the food supply to the population of West Berlin, an act of oppression which was defeated by the "candy bombers" of the American and British air forces. The foundation of the Federal Republic of Germany (FRG) in September 1949 and of the German Democratic Republic (GDR) in October of the same year confirmed the division. From then on, the West Berliners lived on a more or less federal republican island surrounded by the GDR, while the East Berliners were once again residents of the capital. ■ The leadership of East Germany was little bothered by the fact that East Berlin, due to its occupied status, was not an integral part of the GDR. Nor did it matter to them that their state called itself democratic, without actually being so. The "Sozialistische Einheitspartei Deutschlands" (SED Socialist Unity Party of Germany) let many truths go unnoticed, although they sang the great song of infallibility. The anthem "The party, the party, it is always right" rang out for the first time in 1950, and was to be sung innumerable times, as if the ruling powers continually wanted to reassure themselves that their way was the right one. Quite the opposite was proven when the people started to "vote with their feet". Up to the time of the construction of the Wall in 1961, 2.6 million people fled to West Germany, which in addition to the ideological damage also created economic problems for the "workers' and farmers' state" as a result of the loss of labour. The GDR leadership tried to counteract this emigration by closing off the inner German border from 1952 by prohibited areas, fences and guard posts, but this only lead to the escape routes becoming concentrated in the divided city of Berlin. Many citizens of other Eastern Bloc states also absconded to the West over the inner-city demarcation line. ■ The state security forces had long been toying with the idea of closing off these "boltholes" in the middle of Berlin with a wall. The planning proceeded under the strictest secrecy, which the First Secretary of the Central Committee of the SED, Walter Ulbricht, on one occasion took a little too seriously. On 15th June 1961, he stated "Nobody has any intention of building a wall", although nobody had yet mentioned such a border construction in public. Many might therefore have wondered why he chose to make such a denial at this time. ■ And so, in the first two weeks of August of the year 1961, over 47,000 people fled. And just in time too, for on the night of the 12th–13th August 1961, units of the National People's Army, the Border Police and the People's Police and other members of the armed forces moved in to close the sector border with West Berlin. Two days later, on 15th August, builders set to work, while western news agencies in the free sector of Berlin took up position. Camera teams and photographers recorded some dramatic scenes, such as the flight of one East German soldier, who escaped to freedom by taking a flying leap over the barbed wire, or the woman who climbed out of the window of a house standing on the border. Two men attempted to pull her back, but then gave up. Down below, the West Berlin Fire Brigade waited with an outstretched jumping blanket. These images could of course not be seen on East German television. Here other, more edifying things went out over the ether, such as the popular entertainment programme "Da lacht der Bär", which until 1965 was broadcast once per month from the East Berlin "Friedrichstadtpalast". Before the construction of the wall, the presenters had been canvassing for a unified Germany, but now they avoided this subject. Perhaps the words about the laughing bear alluded to the title of this programme? ■ The GDR leadership walled in West Berlin in order to keep its own population in. Escape attempts frequently ended fatally. The first shots were heard on 24th August 1961. They hit the 24-year old Günther Litfin, as he attempted to swim through the Berlin-Spandau shipping canal to West Berlin. For the family members of the victims, it must have sounded sheer cynicism when the SED christened the wall the "Anti-fascist protection wall". But the will for freedom could not be broken. Some fugitives escaped by spectacular means, either by digging tunnels under the wall or by flying over the border in home-made aircraft. Others risked the direct route through the border posts, although these were designed so treacherously that they often became a deadly trap. ■ Over many stretches, two walls ran parallel, one a few metres away from the demarcation line, and the other shutting off the residential areas, streets and squares of East Berlin. In the strip

draht auch Wachtürme, um das Areal rund um die Uhr von oben observieren zu können. Nachts sorgten Lampen für taghelles Licht, zudem waren die Mauern weiß gestrichen und im gesamten Gelände Signalanlagen versteckt, die bei Berührung Alarm auslösten, so dass kaum eine Chance bestand, unentdeckt zu bleiben. Schäferhunde waren darauf abgerichtet, auf Eindringlinge Jagd zu machen, und Grenzposten angewiesen, von der Schusswaffe Gebrauch zu machen. Wie viele Flüchtlinge durch den Schießbefehl ums Leben kamen, ist bis heute nicht endgültig geklärt. In einer aktuellen Studie konnten 125 Fälle nachgewiesen werden. Doch scheint die Zahl der Opfer um einiges höher zu liegen. Diejenigen, die den Fluchtversuch überlebten, wurden zu mehrjährigen Gefängnisstrafen verurteilt. ■ Zunächst bestand die Mauer aus 30 cm dicken Steinblöcken. Da diese Konstruktion Sprengstoffanschlägen und Fahrzeugdurchbrüchen nicht stand hielt, wurden von 1963 an aufeinander geschichtete Betonplatten verwendet. Die Mauerstärke betrug nun einen Meter. 1968 folgte die dritte Bauart, bei der man zu einer geringeren Wandbreite zurückkehrte. Nun kamen waagerecht übereinander gesetzte Betonteile mit einer Tiefe von 10 cm zum Einsatz, außerdem ein Rohraufsatz als Abschluss, um beim Überklettern keinen Halt zu bieten. ■ Die Mauer war nun 3,60 m hoch und schirmte so den Osten vom Westen ab. Zu dieser Zeit entwickelte sich bereits das Phänomen des Mauertourismus: Jeder, der Westberlin besuchte, wollte nicht nur den Kurfürstendamm entlang schlendern oder die Gedächtniskirche besichtigen, sondern auch die berühmt-berüchtigte Mauer sehen. Es gab Hochstände, von denen man einen Blick nach „drüben" werfen konnte. Während die Touristen gen Osten fotografierten, zielten die Grenzschützer der DDR aus den Wachtürmen mit ihren Ferngläsern nach Westen. Auch Staatsmänner, die durch den Besuch der Grenze ihre Solidarität mit dem eingemauerten und geteilten Berlin bekundeten, wurden misstrauisch ins Visier genommen. So auch der Präsident der Vereinigten Staaten John F. Kennedy, der am 26. Juni 1963 gemeinsam mit Bundeskanzler Konrad Adenauer und dem Regierenden Bürgermeister Willy Brandt die Sperren am Brandenburger Tor und am Checkpoint Charlie besichtigte. Die Bilder seines Berlinbesuchs gingen um die Welt – zusammen mit der berühmten Rede vor dem Schöneberger Rathaus, in der Kennedy bekannte: „Ich bin ein Berliner". Ein Zeichen der Hoffnung; aber auf der DDR-Seite lagen schon die Materialien zum Ausbau der Mauer bereit. ■ 1963 war die Wand noch keine 25 km lang, sie sollte aber mehrfach erweitert werden und erreichte zuletzt eine Ausdehnung von über 100 km. Hinzu kamen Metallzäune, welche die übrigen Grenzabschnitte sicherten. Das Bauwerk war bereits zweimal erneuert worden, als 1975 wieder Arbeitstrupps anrückten. Die waagrecht liegenden Betonplatten wurden durch senkrechte, in Reih und Glied stehende ersetzt. Nun war der „Schutzwall" 3,80 bis 4,10 m hoch und 16 cm dick. In Übereinstimmung mit dem militärischen Wettrüsten zwischen Ost und West wurde auch die Grenze hochgerüstet. ■ Wer immer die vierte Bauart für die Mauer geplant hatte, eines hatte er offenbar nicht bedacht: Die Betonplatten waren so breit und glatt, überdies noch weiß grundiert und fugenlos miteinander verbunden, dass sie geradewegs dazu einluden, bemalt und besprüht zu werden. Selbstverständlich konnte dies nicht von beiden Seiten erfolgen, sondern nur von der Seite aus, die Westberlin zugewandt war. Die Mauer stand jedoch nicht direkt an der Grenzlinie, sondern auf einem Geländestreifen, der schon zur DDR gehörte und eigentlich nicht betreten werden durfte. Eben dieses schmale Niemandsland schützte die mit Farbe anrückenden westlichen Grenzgänger. Gelegentlich ließ sich zwar das Wachpersonal auf dieser Seite der Mauer blicken. Doch hatten die Graffitimaler, die sich, juristisch gesehen, mindestens der Sachbeschädigung schuldig machten, leichtes Spiel: Um einer möglichen Verhaftung zu entgehen, genügte ein Sprung zurück in den Westen. So wurden sie immer wagemutiger und hinterließen bald nicht nur im Schutz der Dunkelheit, sondern auch am Tag ihre Spuren. ■ Einer hinterließ einen Gruß, ein anderer bewies sich als „Picasso on the street", wieder ein anderer rief zum „Ungehorsam" gegen die „Pershing 2" auf. Und einer malte einen Mauerdurchbruch, so als ob hier jemand von Ost- nach Westberlin geflohen sei. Die fiktive Öffnung – an der Stelle, an der sich auch der Spruch vom lachenden Bären befand – gab den Blick auf die real existierende Zone hinter der Mauer frei. In einem weiteren Graffiti starrte aus einer Maueröffnung ein Totenkopf als eindringliche Anklage. Andere Bilder berichteten von individuellen Lebenswelten, manchmal voller Ironie und Humor, manchmal aber auch sehr ernst und nachdenklich. Oder sie karikierten und kommentierten aktuelle politische Ereignisse. Der Brutalität des Ortes war die Freiheit von Gedanken und Bildern entgegengesetzt. Dies drückte sich auf sehr unterschiedliche Weise in Motiven aus, welche die Mauer – im eigentlichen Wortsinn – missachten. Die Graffiti machten den Betonriegel nicht erträglicher, aber sie setzten Zeichen gegen die Allgegenwart der Grenze. ■ Viele Mauersprayer lebten im alternativen Kreuzberg, in dem jeder die Grenzwand tagtäglich vor Augen hatte. Andere kamen von weit her – so wie der New Yorker Künstler Keith Haring, der 1986 einhundert Meter am Checkpoint Charlie als Protest gegen die „Lächerlichkeit von Grenzen und Feindschaft" bemalte. Dass er dabei die Graffiti anderer überdeckte und dass dies in der Berliner Sprayerszene auf einigen Unmut stieß, sei hier nur nebenbei erwähnt. Der Kampf um attraktive Wandflächen war entbrannt. Die Graffiti „kannibalisierten" sich gegenseitig. ■ Ob aber in der Machtzentrale der DDR die Frage erörtert wurde, sämtliche Bilder und Aufschriften durch einen Anstrich zu tilgen? Genutzt hätte dies sicher wenig. Denn kaum wäre die Farbe trocken gewesen, hätten die Sprayer aus dem Westen das Monument der politischen Unfreiheit wieder zu einem Ort der Freiheit gemacht.

of land between them stood fences of barbed wire, and also watchtowers, so as to be able to observe the area from above all round the clock. Searchlights turned the night into day; the walls were also painted white, and signal systems were concealed everywhere, which set off the alarm on contact, so that there was hardly any chance of remaining undiscovered. Guard dogs were trained to hunt intruders, and border posts ordered to make use of their firearms. Even today, it has not been definitively determined how many fugitives lost their life as a result of this order to "shoot on sight". A current study has been able to confirm 125 cases, although the number of victims appears to be somewhat higher. Those who survived an attempted escape were sentenced to long prison terms. ■ The wall was initially constructed of 30 cm thick stone blocks. Since this construction could not withstand explosive attacks or being rammed by vehicles, this was progressively replaced from 1963 by overlapping concrete slabs. The wall's thickness was increased to one metre. This was followed in 1968 by a third type of construction, which returned to a lower wall thickness. Horizontally overlapping concrete slabs with a depth of 10 cm were now used, together with a semi-circular section of piping on top, in order to offer no hold to anyone attempting to climb the wall. ■ The wall was now 3.60 m high and effectively screened off the East from the West. At this time, the phenomenon of "wall tourism" was already developing: everyone who visited West Berlin not only wanted to stroll along the Kurfürstendamm or visit the Memorial Church, but also to see the famous and notorious wall. There were even raised stands, from where one could obtain a view of the "other side". While the tourists took photographs of the East, the border guards of the GDR looked back into the West from the watchtowers through their binoculars. Statesmen who wanted to express their solidarity with the walled-in and divided Berlin by visiting the border were also regarded suspiciously through the sights. Amongst them was the President of the United States, John F. Kennedy, who on 26th June 1963, together with the West German Chancellor Konrad Adenauer and Mayor Willy Brandt, visited the barriers at the Brandenburg Gate and Checkpoint Charlie. These images were flashed around the world – together with the famous speech in front of the Schöneberg Town Hall, in which Kennedy professed: "I am a Berliner". A sign of hope; but on the GDR side, the materials for extending the wall already lay ready. ■ By 1963, the wall was still not yet 25 km long, although it was to be extended several times, finally reaching a length of over 100 km. This was augmented by metal fences, which secured the remaining sections of the border. The wall had already been replaced twice when labour gangs turned up again in 1975. The horizontal concrete slabs were replaced by vertical slabs, standing in rank and file, creating a wall that was now 3.80 to 4.10 m in height and 16 cm thick. In concert with the military arms race between the East and West, the border fortifications were also upgraded. ■ Whoever had planned the fourth type of construction for the wall had clearly failed to consider one thing: The concrete slabs were so wide and smooth, and also primed in white paint and connected seamlessly with each other, that they simply begged to be painted and sprayed with graffiti. Of course this could not be done from both sides, but only from the side facing West Berlin. The wall did not stand directly on the border line, but on a strip of land which belonged to the GDR, and was strictly off-limits. It was exactly this narrow no-man's-land which protected the western border-crossers armed with spray cans and tubes of paint. The guards were occasionally seen on this side of the wall. But the graffiti artists, who legally speaking were at least responsible for the material damage, were not worried: all they had to do was jump back into the West in order to avoid possible arrest. They now became increasingly daring, carrying out their artwork not only under cover of darkness, but also during the day. ■ One left behind a greeting, another proved to be a "Picasso on the street", while yet another called for "disobedience" against the "Peshing 2". And another even painted a hole in the wall, as if someone had here fled from East Berlin into the West. This fake opening – at the point where the words about the laughing bear were also found – showed a view of the zone as it actually existed behind the wall. In another piece of graffiti, a skull stared out of an opening in the wall, a token of mute accusation. Other images told of individual experiences, sometimes full of irony and humour, sometimes however also very serious and thoughtful. Or they caricatured and commented on current political events. The brutality of the place was contrasted with the freedom of thought and imagery. This was expressed in very different ways in motifs which flouted the wall in the actual sense of the word. The graffiti did not make the concrete slabs any more tolerable, but it did express the Berliners' objection to the omnipresence of the border. ■ Many wall artists lived in the Kreuzberg district, in which nobody could avoid seeing the wall everyday. Others came from further afield, such as the New York artist Keith Haring, who in 1986 painted a 100 m area of the wall at Checkpoint Charley as a protest against the "ludicrousness of borders and hostility". It should be mentioned no more than incidentally that he thereby covered the graffiti applied by others, thereby causing no little discontent amongst the Berlin sprayer scene. A struggle flared up for attractive wall areas. The graffiti works now "cannibalised" each other. ■ Was the question of painting over the graffiti ever considered in the corridors of power of the GDR? This would certainly have been of little use, since the paint would hardly have been dry, before new images would have turned this monument to political oppression back into a place of artistic freedom. ■ For this reason too, the words

■ Auch deshalb hatte der Spruch vom lachenden Bären seine Berechtigung: Wie so vieles andere, was sich nicht aufhalten oder verhindern ließ, führte die Graffiti die Abschottungspolitik der Regierungspartei der DDR ad absurdum. Die SED hätte die Zeichen der Zeit schon früh erkennen und darauf reagieren können, so wie der Verbündete im Osten. Als aber Michail Gorbatschow in den achtziger Jahren von „Perestroika" und „Glasnost" sprach, hüllte sich Erich Honecker in eisiges Schweigen. Der „Generalsekretär des Zentralkomitees der Sozialistischen Einheitspartei Deutschlands und Staatsratsvorsitzende der Deutschen Demokratischen Republik", wie die DDR-Nachrichten jedes Mal formelhaft wiederholten, wenn sie über ihn berichteten, wollte von Reformen nichts wissen. Er war und blieb uneinsichtig, was wohl auch daran lag, dass er als ZK-Sekretär für Sicherheitsfragen die Planung und Durchführung des Mauerbaus politisch verantwortet hatte. So tönte er noch am 19. Januar 1989: „Die Mauer wird in fünfzig und auch in hundert Jahren noch bestehen bleiben, wenn die dazu vorhandenen Gründe noch nicht beseitigt sind". Wenige Wochen später, am 6. Februar 1989, fielen an der Grenze wieder tödliche Schüsse, diesmal allerdings das letzte Mal. ■ Mit dem Ruf „Wir sind das Volk" ging die Bevölkerung im September 1989 auf die Straße, um Recht und Freiheit für sich einzufordern. Während sich die Demonstrationen zu Massenprotesten ausweiteten – so am 4. November mit einer Million Teilnehmern in Ostberlin – geriet die SED durch die Reformpolitik Ungarns und der Tschechoslowakei zusätzlich unter Druck. Beide Länder wurden von ausreisewilligen DDR-Bürgern geradezu überrannt, als sie ihre Grenzen nach Westen öffneten. Die SED glaubte die Krise mit einem neuen Ausreisegesetz bewältigen zu können. Doch als das Politbüromitglied Günter Schabowski am 9. November 1989 in einer Pressekonferenz darüber berichtete, brauchte es nur weniger Worte, um den Stein ins Rollen, die Mauer zum Einsturz zu bringen. „Wann tritt das in Kraft?" wurde von einem Journalisten gefragt. „Das tritt nach meiner Kenntnis ... ist das sofort, unverzüglich" lautete die Antwort. ■ Rundfunk- und Fernsehsender im Westen meldeten noch am selben Tag die Mauer sei „offen" und lösten so einen Ansturm der Ostberliner auf die unvorbereiteten innerstädtischen Grenzübergänge aus. An der Bornholmer Straße entschied sich ein Offizier für das einzig Richtige und öffnete den Grenzübergang. Es war eine halbe Stunde vor Mitternacht. Bald feierte ganz Berlin. Nun gingen Bilder der Freude um die Welt. Ob dies der Unbekannte geahnt hatte, als er auf die Mauer die Worte vom lachenden Bären schrieb? ■ Noch war die Stadt aber nicht wiedervereint. Noch wurde sie von der Mauer geteilt, wenngleich sich die eine oder andere Grenzsoldat bereits die Frage gestellt haben dürfte, wie lange er seinen Dienst noch ausüben würde. Denn das Ende der Grenze schien nur eine Frage der Zeit. Dies ahnten auch die „Mauerspechte", die mit Hammer und Meißel Erinnerungsstücke – oder besser Trophäen – aus der Wand brachen. ■ Mit Inkrafttreten der Währungsunion am 1. Juli 1990 wurden Bewachung und Grenzkontrollen eingestellt. Am 13. Juli 1990 begannen DDR-Soldaten mit dem Abbau, begleitet vom Applaus der Berliner Bevölkerung, die mit dem Mauerfall auch das Ende der DDR beklatschte. Nach dem 3. Oktober führten Pioniere der Bundeswehr den Abbruch weiter. Im innerstädtischen Bereich wurde die Maßnahme offiziell am 30. November 1990 beendet, während die äußeren Grenzanlagen bis Ende 1991 fielen. Bald verschwanden auch die breiten Schneisen, die das Bauwerk geschlagen hatte. Das wieder vereinte Berlin, nun Hauptstadt und Regierungssitz des einigen Deutschlands, nutzte das frühere Grenzland für seinen Auf- und Ausbau. An den Orten, die einst durch Betonabsperrungen und Stacheldraht geprägt waren, entstanden neue Plätze und Grünanlagen oder wuchsen Wohn- und Bürohäuser in die Höhe. Daneben blieben vereinzelt noch Mauersegmente stehen, nicht weil sie vergessen wurden, sondern weil man sie als Orte der mahnenden Erinnerung erhalten wollte. Darüber wurde kontrovers diskutiert, doch wird heute wohl niemand mehr bezweifeln, dass diese Entscheidung richtig und angesichts manch verklärender Erinnerung auch notwendig war. Die Relikte des Kalten Krieges wurden unter Denkmalschutz gestellt und bilden nun Anschauungsstoff für Schulklassen und Touristen, die auf „Mauerrundgängen" die Irrwege deutscher Geschichte erkunden. ■ Teile der Mauer finden sich heute als Dokumente der Zeitgeschichte auch außerhalb Berlins, etwa im Haus der Geschichte in Bonn, im Englischen Garten in München, im Imperial War Museum in London sowie beim Sitz der Vereinten Nationen in New York. Andere gelangten in den Kunsthandel. Die Mauergraffiti war in der Wendezeit heiß begehrt. Sogar die DDR hatte in ihren letzten Tagen daraus noch Kapital geschlagen, indem sie bemalte Segmente über eine Außenhandelsfirma verkaufte. Die Mauermaler gingen bei diesen Geschäften zunächst leer aus, konnten aber später gerichtlich Vergütungsansprüche durchsetzen. 1990 fanden in Berlin und Monaco viel beachtete Versteigerungen von Mauersegmenten statt. Derweil machte sich im selben Jahr eine Gruppe von Künstlern daran, die erhaltene Hinterlandmauer in der Mühlenstraße entlang der Spree als East Side Gallery zu bemalen – fast so als wollte man die Zeit subversiver Mauerkunst zurückholen. ■ Wie viele Mauerteile auch heute noch in Berlin und anderswo existieren mögen: Die Brutalität, mit der die Mauer als Grenze durch Berlin geschlagen wurde, tritt nirgends deutlicher als in den Bilddokumenten hervor. Dies gilt in besonderem Maße für die Aufnahmen von Armin Lindauer in diesem Buch. Neben der subversiven Kreativität der Graffiti führen sie uns auch die Brutalität und Absurdität des „antifaschistischen Schutzwalls" vor Augen. Dies macht sie zu einem beeindruckenden Dokument des Anfangs vom Ende der Mauer.

about the laughing bear were justified: like so many other things which cannot be stopped or prevented, the graffiti depicted as absurd the segregation policy of the ruling party of the GDR. The SED could have been able to recognise the signs of the times at an early stage and react accordingly, just as their ally in the East. But when Mikhail Gorbachev began to talk of "perestroika" and "glasnost" in the 1980's, Erich Honecker maintained an icy silence. The "General Secretary of the Central Committee of the Socialist Unity Party of Germany and Chairman of the State Council of the German Democratic Republic", as the GDR news agency repeated formally on every occasion when reporting about him, wanted to hear nothing about reform. He was and remained obdurate, which was probably also due to the fact that as Central Committee Secretary for Security, he was politically responsible for the planning and construction of the wall. He accordingly announced on 19th January 1989: "The wall will still be standing in 50 or even 100 years time, if the causes for its construction have not been rectified". A few weeks later, on 6th February 1989, fatal shots were once again fired at the border, although for the last time. ■ With the call "We are the people", the population turned out onto the street in September 1989 to reclaim their right and freedom. As the demonstrations escalated to mass protests – on 4th November around one million people gathered in East Berlin – the SED came under further pressure due to the reform policies of Hungary and Czechoslovakia. Both countries were overrun by GDR citizens wanting to leave the country when they opened their borders to the West. The SED believed that it could overcome the crisis with a new emigration law. But when Politburo member Günter Schabowski reported this move in a press conference on 9th November 1989, it only needed a few words in order to set the ball rolling to tear down the wall. "When will the law come into force?" asked one journalist. "As far as I am aware, it comes into force… now, immediately" came the answer. ■ On the same day, radio and TV stations in the West announced that the wall was "open", thereby causing a rush of East Berliners to the unprepared inner-city border crossings. At the Bornholmer Straße, one officer decided to do the only right thing, and opened the border crossing. It was half an hour before midnight. Soon the whole of Berlin was celebrating. Pictures of the rejoicing went round the world. Had he suspected this, the unknown graffiti artist, when he wrote the words about the laughing bear on the wall? ■ But the city was not yet reunited. It was still divided by the wall, even though one or other of the border guards had probably already asked the question of how long he should stick to his post. For the end of the border now seemed only a question of time. This was also anticipated by the "wall-peckers", who with hammers and chisels quickly started to chip mementos – or to put it better trophies – out of the wall. ■ With the coming into effect of the currency union on 1st July 1990, surveillance and border controls were discontinued. On 13th July 1990, GDR troops began the demolition of the wall, spurred on by the applause of Berlin's population, who with the removal of the wall were also celebrating the end of the GDR. After 3rd October, pioneers of the West German Army continued with the demolition. In the inner-city area, the work was officially completed on 30th November 1990, while the remaining border posts were all taken down by the end of 1991. The wide swathes of land left empty by the wall soon also disappeared. The reunited Berlin, now the capital and seat of government of a single Germany, used the former border land for its reconstruction work. At the places where concrete barriers and barbed wire fences had once stood, new squares and parks were laid out, or new residential and office buildings constructed. Around them, isolated segments of the wall remained standing, not because they had been forgotten, but because it was decided to leave them as salutary reminders of the wall. This caused much controversial discussion, but today probably nobody doubts that this decision was right and also necessary as a reminder of the past. The relics of the Cold War were designated as protected monuments and now form sites of interest for school classes and tourists, who on "wall tours" explore the aberrations of German history. ■ Pieces of the wall can today be found as documents of contemporary history outside Berlin, such as in the "Haus der Geschichte" in Bonn, in the English Garden in Munich, in the Imperial War Museum in London and at the headquarters of the United Nations in New York. Others entered into circulation in the art trade. The wall art was much sought-after following the demolition of the wall. Even the GDR had in its last days made capital out of it, by selling painted sections through an export company. The wall artists initially made nothing from this business, although they were later able to assert their payment claims legally. Well-attended auctions of wall art were held in 1990 in Berlin and Monaco. Meanwhile, in the same year, a group of artists set about painting the Hinterland wall in the Mühlenstraße along the Spree as the East Side Gallery, almost as if wanting to recall the time of the subversive wall art. ■ However many pieces of the wall may still exist today in Berlin and elsewhere: The brutality with which the Wall was thrown up as a border through Berlin appears nowhere more clearly than in the pictorial documents. This applies particularly to the pictures of Armin Lindauer reproduced in this book. In addition to the subversive creativity of the graffiti, they also depict to us the brutality and absurdity of the "antifascist protection wall", making them an impressive document of the beginning of the end of the Wall.

1984–86 Bernauer Straße →

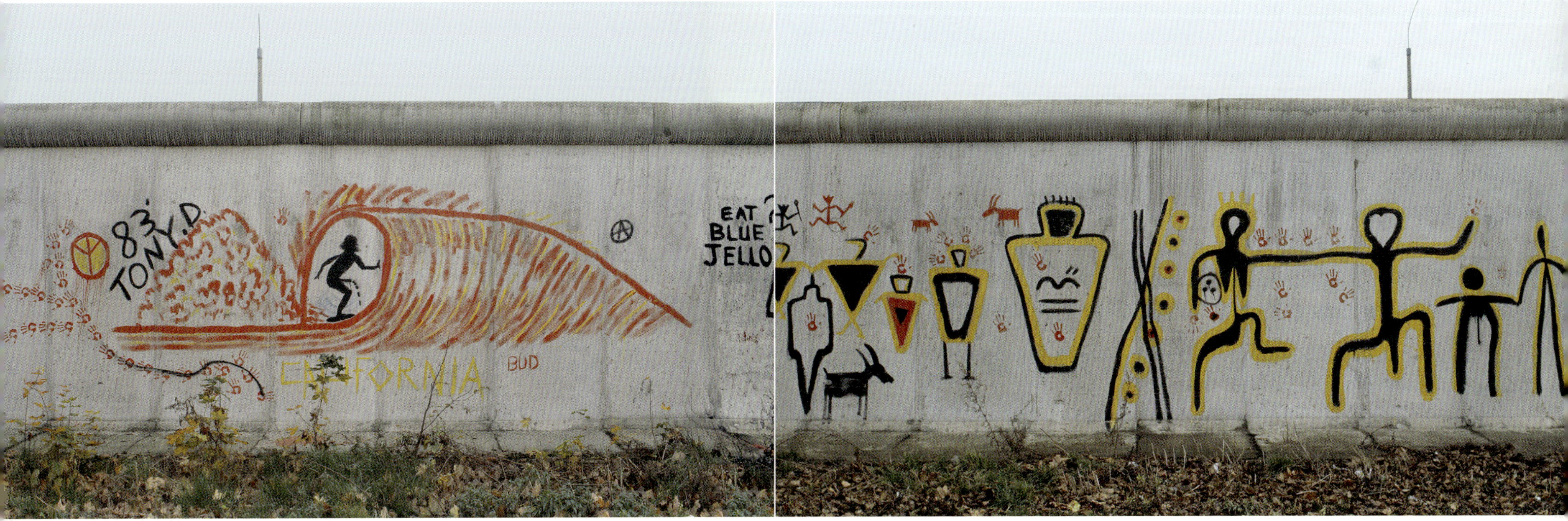
83
TONY.D
EAT
BLUE
JELLO
BUD

1984–86 Bernauer Straße →

Wohnhaus in Ost-Berlin
Residential block in East Berlin

1984–86 Bernauer Straße →

Evangelische Versöhnungskirche. Sie stand auf dem so genannten Todesstreifen und wurde am 28. Januar 1985 gesprengt.
The Evangelist Church of the Reconciliation. This stood on the so-called death strip, and was demolished on 28th January 1985.

1984–86 Ebertstraße, nahe Reichstag *near the Reichstag* →

Spionagetür (auch Schlupftor) in der Berliner Mauer, welche die Grenztruppen der DDR oder Spione des Ministeriums für Staatssicherheit benutzten, um unbemerkt in den Westen zu gelangen.
A spy door in the Berlin Wall used by the GDR border scouts to enter West Berlin unnoticed.

1984–86 Ebertstraße, nahe Reichstag *near the Reichstag* →

1984–86 Stresemannstraße →

Reichstagsgebäude, seit 1999 Sitz des Deutschen Bundestages.
The Reichstag building, seat of the German government since 1999.

JOBOXERS COMMUNISTS ARE JUST PART-TIME WORKERS
SCHEISS BULLE

1984–86 Niederkirchnerstraße, nahe Martin-Gropius-Bau *near the Martin Gropius Building* →

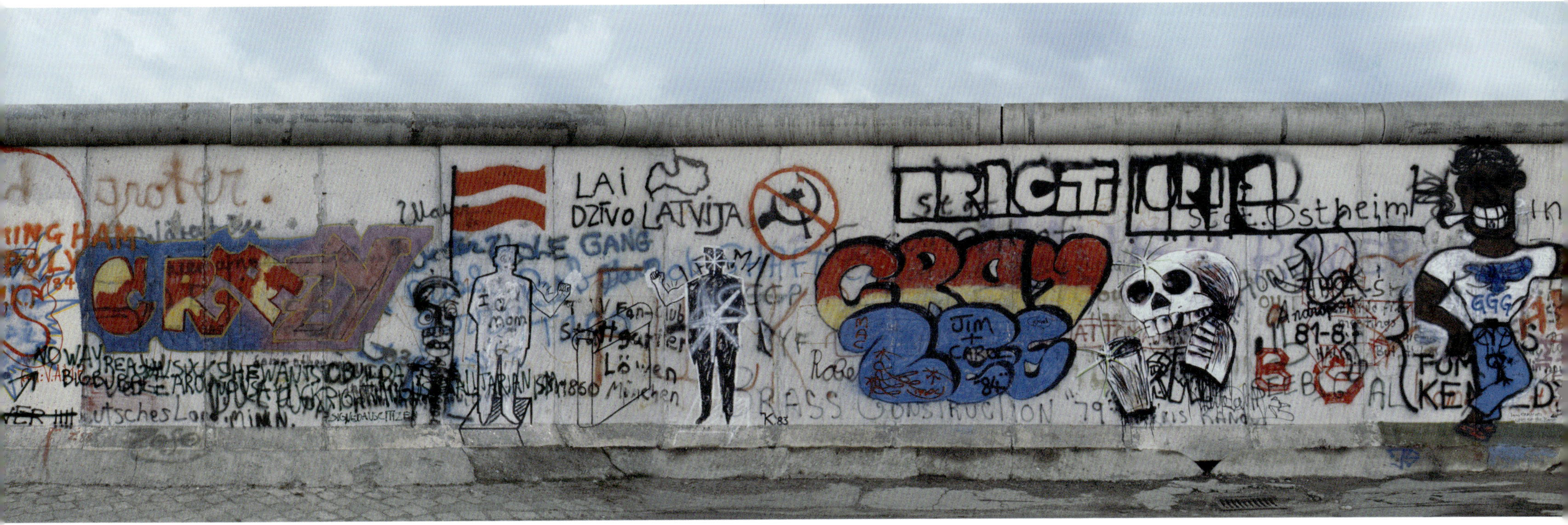

1984–86 Niederkirchnerstraße, nahe Martin-Gropius-Bau *near the Martin Gropius Building* →

Zephyr, New Yorker Graffiti-Maler / *New York graffiti artist*

NOAH AND THE AARDVARKS! '84

1984–86 Niederkirchnerstraße, nahe Martin-Gropius-Bau *near the Martin Gropius Building* →

Peter Weiss →

← Peter Weiss

Jonathan Borowski „Running Man", 1982

Peter Weiss →

1984–86 Niederkirchnerstraße, nahe Martin-Gropius-Bau *near the Martin Gropius Building* →

Jonathan Borowski „Running Man", 1982 ← Peter Weiss →

Der ehemalige Preußische Landtag (1899 bis 1934). Nach dem Fall der Berliner Mauer wird er vollständig renoviert und ist seit April 1993 das Abgeordnetenhaus von Berlin.
The former Prussian Landtag (1899 to 1934). Following the fall of the Berlin Wall, it was completely renovated, and since April 1993 has been the Berlin House of Representatives.

← Peter Weiss

1984–86 Niederkirchnerstraße, nahe Martin-Gropius-Bau *near the Martin Gropius Building* →

Der ehemalige Preußische Landtag (1899 bis 1934). Nach dem Fall der Berliner Mauer wird er vollständig renoviert und ist seit April 1993 das Abgeordnetenhaus von Berlin.
The former Prussian Landtag (1899 to 1934). Following the fall of the Berlin Wall, it was completely renovated, and since April 1993 has been the Berlin House of Representatives.

1984–86 Niederkirchnerstraße, nahe Martin-Gropius-Bau *near the Martin Gropius Building* →

1984–86 Niederkirchnerstraße, Ecke Wilhelmstraße *corner of Wilhelmstraße* →

Der ehemalige Preußische Landtag (1899 bis 1934). Nach dem Fall der Berliner Mauer wird er vollständig renoviert und ist seit April 1993 das Abgeordnetenhaus von Berlin.
The former Prussian Landtag (1899 to 1934). Following the fall of the Berlin Wall, it was completely renovated, and since April 1993 has been the Berlin House of Representatives.

Ehemals Reichsluftfahrtministerium, heute Bundesministerium für Finanzen
Formerly the Reich Air Transport Ministry, today the Federal Ministry of Finance

Anarchie ist die höchste Form der Demokratie

1984–86 Zimmerstraße, zwischen Friedrich- und Charlottenstraße *between Friedrichstraße and Charlottenstraße* →

Vordergebäude der ehemaligen Markthalle 3, 1884 bis 86 erbaut (Zimmerstraße 90/91).
Anterior building of the former Market Hall 3, constructed from 1884 to 86.

Gebäudekomplex des Zentralverlages der NSDAP, erbaut in den 20er Jahren. Seit 1955 wird das Haus vom Parteiverlag der SED genutzt. Bis 1980 werden dort nahezu alle Tageszeitungen Ost-Berlins gedruckt.
Building complex of the central publishing house of the NSDAP, built in the 1920's. Since 1955 the building has been used by the party printers of the SED. Until 1980, almost all daily newspapers of East Berlin were printed here.

1984–86 Zimmerstraße, zwischen Wilhelm- und Friedrichstraße *between Wilhelmstraße and Friedrichstraße* →

Geschäftshaus Zimmerstraße 79/80, erbaut 1913/14.
Office building at Zimmerstraße 79/80, built 1913/14.

Felix und Vera

Christophe Bouchet, Thierry Noir

1984–86 Zimmerstraße, Ecke Charlottenstraße *corner of Charlottenstraße* →

1984–86 Axel-Springer-Straße, ehemals Lindenstraße *formerly Lindenstraße* →

Hochhäuser der Leipziger Straße
High-rise blocks on Leipziger Straße

1984–86 Axel-Springer-Straße, ehemals Lindenstraße *formerly Lindenstraße* →

Hochhäuser an der Leipziger Straße
High-rise blocks on Leipziger Straße

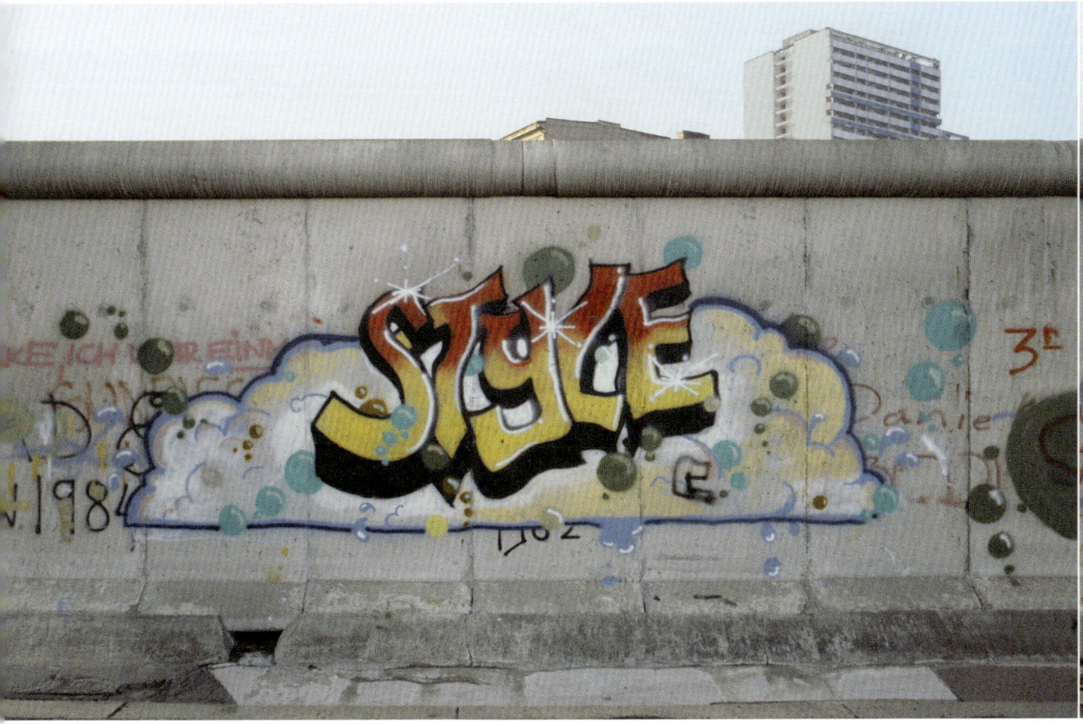
STYLE

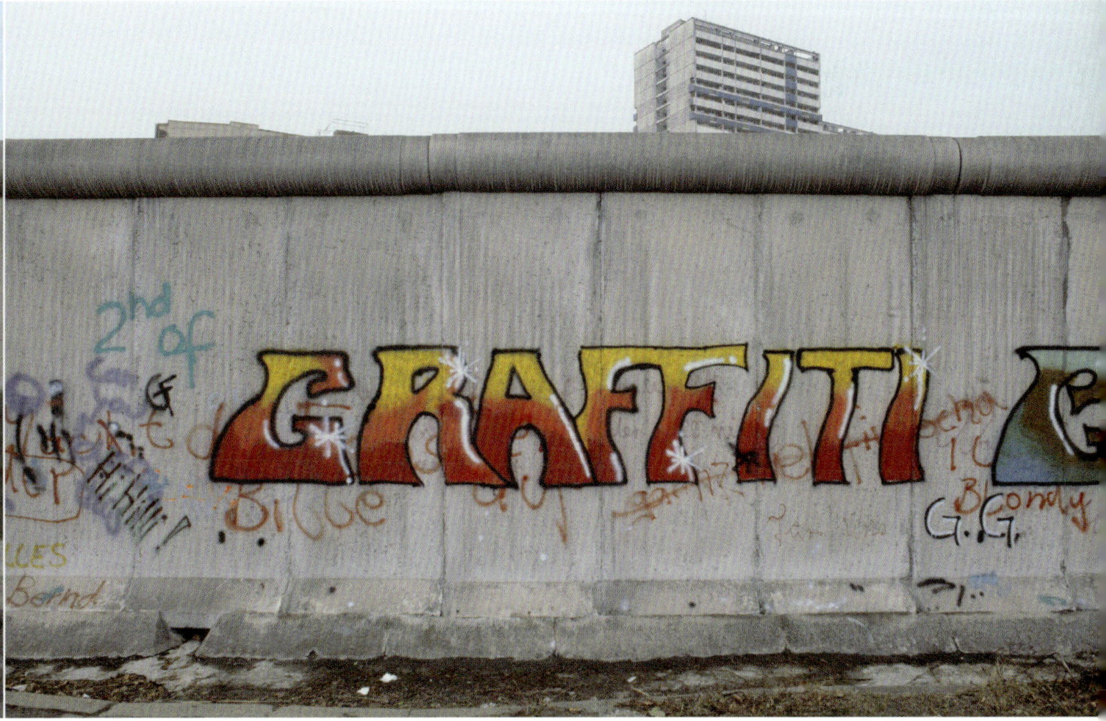
2nd of
GRAFFITI
G.G.

1984–86 Sebastianstraße →

"ON WISCONSIN"

BERLIN 84

1984–86 Luckauer Straße, Waldemarstraße →

Uli →

← Uli

1984–86 Luckauer Straße, Waldemarstraße →

Uli →

← Uli

1984 – 86 Luckauer Straße, Waldemarstraße →

Uli, Thierry Noir →   ← Uli, Thierry Noir

46 | 47

Tel: 651156
KOLLEKTIV
"WILDER
HAMMER"
Keine

EDGAR
LET ME
PAINT
DIE WITH THE WALL
MBL '84
FREIHEIT
für die
IWF

1984–86 Bethaniendamm →

Thierry Noir

Christophe Bouchet

1984–86 Bethaniendamm →

Thierry Noir „Gebrüder Arbeit"

Christophe Bouchet

Christophe Bouchet   Thierry Noir   Christophe Bouchet, Thierry Noir

1984–86 Bethaniendamm →

Alexander Hacke

Alexander Hacke

Michael Gremenz

1984–86 Bethaniendamm →

Jean-Martin Tandetzki

Jean-Martin Tandetzki

Christian Benazet, Christophe Bouchet

Christian Benazet, Christophe Bouchet   Christophe Bouchet, Michael Gremenz   Christophe Bouchet   Michael Gremenz

1984–86 Bethaniendamm →

Michael Gremenz · Christophe Bouchet · Michael Gremenz · Thierry Noir

Christophe Bouchet

1984–86 Bethaniendamm, zwischen Leuschnerdamm und Adalbertstraße *between Leuschnerdamm and Adalbertstraße* →

Geschäftshaus aus den 20er-Jahren (Engeldamm, Ecke Leuschnerdamm)
Office building dating from the 1920's (Engeldamm, corner of Leuschnerdamm)

Erstes Gewerkschaftshaus Deutschlands, erbaut 1900. 1933 durch die SA besetzt, wird es seit 1945 von der Sowjetunion als Notkrankenhaus genutzt. Später wird es bis 1990 das Städtische Krankenhaus Mitte. (Engelufer 62/64)
The first trade union building in Germany, constructed in 1900. Occupied by the SA in 1933, it was used from 1945 by the Soviet Union as an emergency hospital. Later it became the Central Municipal Hospital until 1990. (Engelufer 62/64)

Christophe Bouchet, Thierry Noir

1984–86 Bethaniendamm, nahe Adalbertstraße *near Adalbertstraße* →

Erstes Gewerkschaftshaus Deutschlands, erbaut 1900. 1933 durch die SA besetzt, wird es seit 1945 von der Sowjetunion als Notkrankenhaus genutzt. Später wird es bis 1990 das Städtische Krankenhaus Mitte. (Engelufer 62/64)
The first trade union building in Germany, constructed in 1900. Occupied by the SA in 1933, it was used from 1945 by the Soviet Union as an emergency hospital. Later it became the Central Municipal Hospital until 1990. (Engelufer 62/64)

Uli →

← Uli

1984–86 Bethaniendamm, nahe Adalbertstraße *near Adalbertstraße* →

Christophe Bouchet, Thierry Noir

Wohnhaus in Ost-Berlin
Residential block in East Berlin

Christophe Bouchet

1984–86 Bethaniendamm, nahe Sankt-Thomas-Kirche *near St. Thomas' Church* →

Links im Anschnitt ist eine Aussichtsplattform zu sehen.
An observation platform can be seen in the left of the view.

Wohnhäuser in Ost-Berlin (Engeldamm, Ecke Melchiorstraße)
Residential block in East Berlin (Engeldamm, corner of Melchiorstraße)

Richard Hambleton · Indiano

1984–86 Bethaniendamm, Ecke Köpenicker Straße *corner of Köpenicker Straße* →

Wohnhaus in Ost-Berlin (Engeldamm, zwischen Melchiorstraße und Köpenicker Straße)
Residential block in East Berlin (Engeldamm, between Melchiorstraße and Köpenicker Straße)

Mark Eins, 1984

1984–86 Lohmühlenstraße →

Das Gebäude gehört zu dem Komplex der Agfa Treptow, erbaut 1873.
Seit 1948 befindet sich hier die Maschinenfabrik Treptow und ab 1960 ein
Sozialistischer Großhandelsbetrieb (SGB). *(Lohmühlenstraße 65–67)*
*Built in 1873, the building belonged to the complex of Agfa Treptow.
The Treptow Machine Factory was accommodated here from 1948, and from
1960 a Socialist Wholesale Business (SGB). (Lohmühlenstraße 65–67)*

1984–86 Lohmühlenstraße →

Das Gebäude gehört zu dem Komplex der Agfa Treptow, erbaut 1873. Seit 1948 befindet sich hier die Maschinenfabrik Treptow und ab 1960 ein Sozialistischer Großhandelsbetrieb (SGB). (Lohmühlenstraße 65–67)
Built in 1873, the building belonged to the complex of Agfa Treptow. The Treptow Machine Factory was accommodated here from 1948, and from 1960 a Socialist Wholesale Business (SGB). (Lohmühlenstraße 65–67)

Martin von Ostrowski

Martin von Ostrowski

Paul Revellio

1991 Potsdamer Platz →

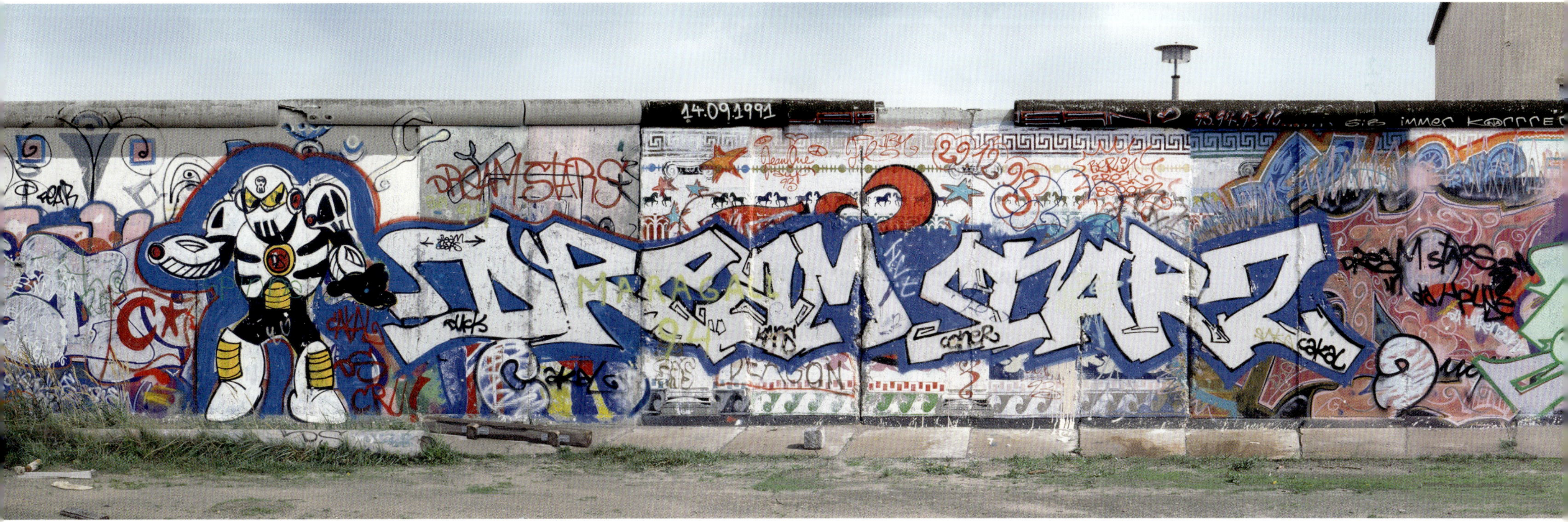

1991 Potsdamer Platz →

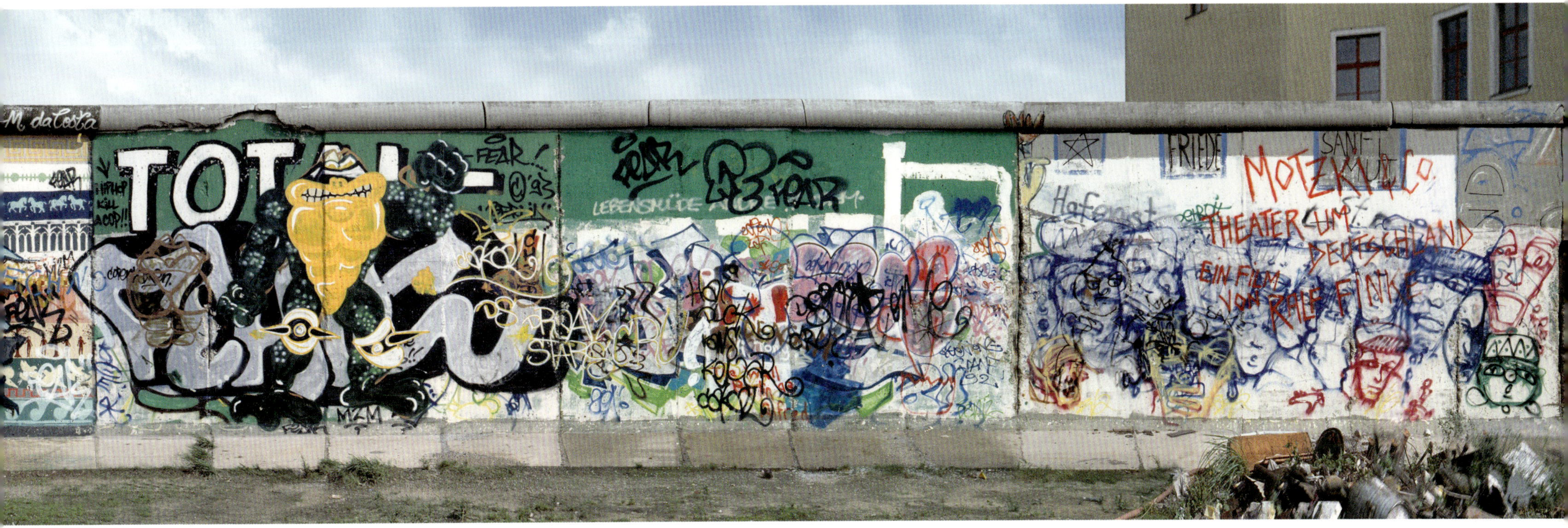

1991 Potsdamer Platz →

...er sieht man auf die Rückseite der Berliner Mauer 1991. Die ehemaligen Grenzan
...ge, der sogenannte Todesstreifen, wird nach dem Mauerfall als Parkplatz genutzt.
...his picture shows the rear side of the Berlin Wall in the year 1991. The former border
...rea, the so-called death strip, was used as a parking area after the fall of the Wall.

1999 Mühlenstraße, East Side Gallery →

Die East Side Gallery ist der größte erhaltene Rest der Grenzanlage der Berliner Mauer mit einer Länge von 1316 m. Sie ist eine sogenannte Hinterlandmauer, und somit nicht die eigentliche Grenze und befindet sich zwischen dem Ostbahnhof und der Oberbaumbrücke entlang der Spree.

The East Side Gallery is the largest preserved stretch of the Berlin Wall, at a length of 1,316 m. This is a so-called Hinterland wall, and therefore not the actual border. It lies between the Ostbahnhof and the Oberbaumbrücke along the Spree.

Ed '96
AUS
HOLLAND
MARCO
TONY
PIRNAIE
amnesty
international
KWIM
THE WALL
Younran Kim

1999 Mühlenstraße, East Side Gallery →

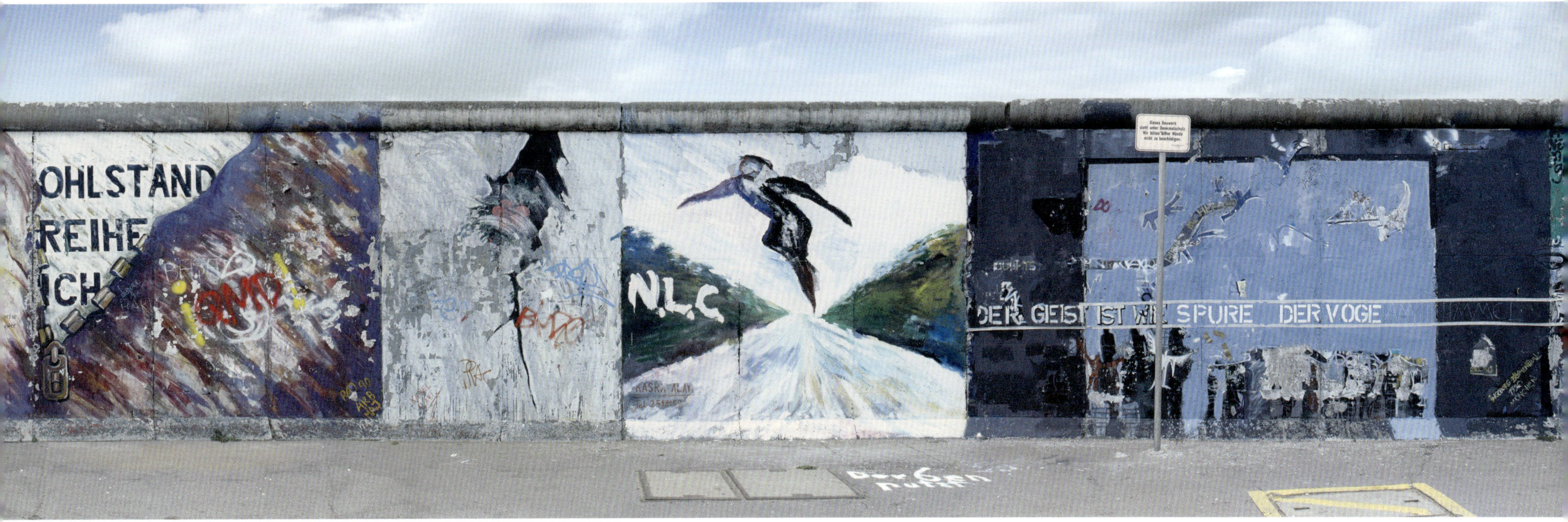
OHLSTAND
REIHE
ICH
N.L.C
DER GEIST IST WIE SPURE DER VOGE

2007 Bernauer Straße, Gedenkstätte und Mahnmal *memorial and monument* →

Gedenkstätte und Mahnmal der Berliner Mauer. Rekonstruktion eines 80 m kurzen Stück Mauer und Grenzland, das durch zwei 6 m hohe Stahlwände eingeschlossen wird.
The memorial and monument of the Berlin Wall. Reconstruction of an 80 m stretch of the Wall with border land, which is enclosed by two 6 m high steel walls.

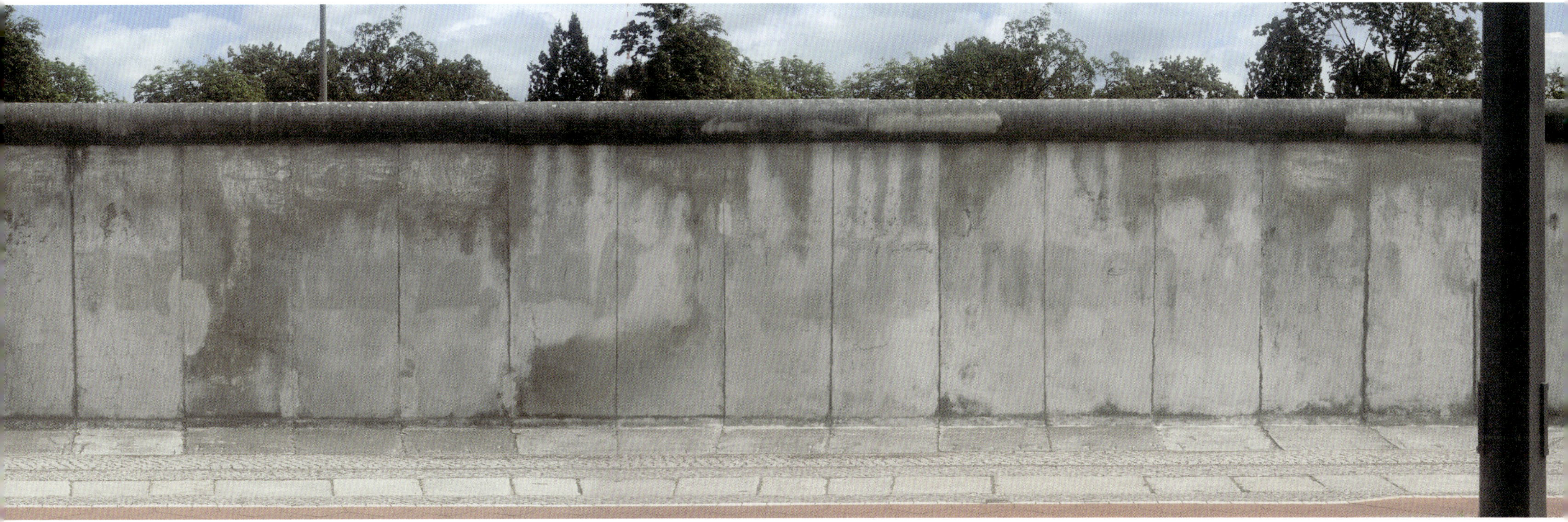

2007 Bernauer Straße, Gedenkstätte und Mahnmal *memorial and monument* →

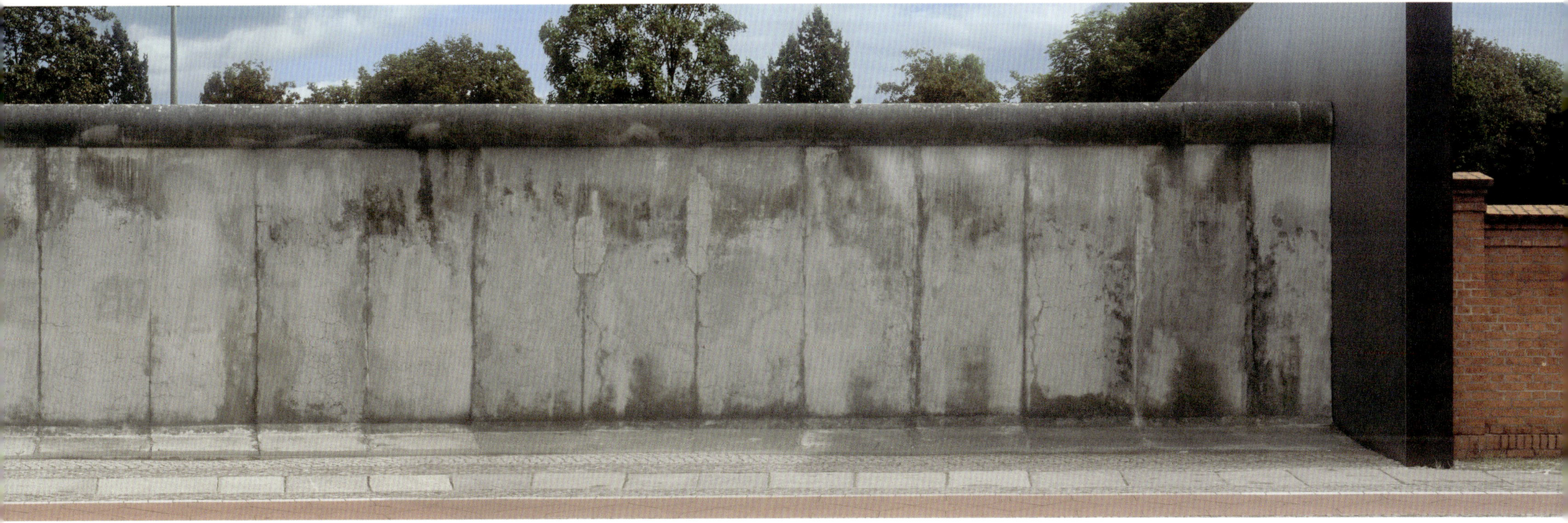

2007 Bernauer Straße →

Rechts des Mahnmals
To the right of the monument

Reststück der Berliner Mauer, deren Armierungseisen von Souvenirjägern freigelegt wurden.
Remains of the Berlin Wall whose steel reinforcements have been exposed by souvenir-hunters.

2007 Bernauer Straße →

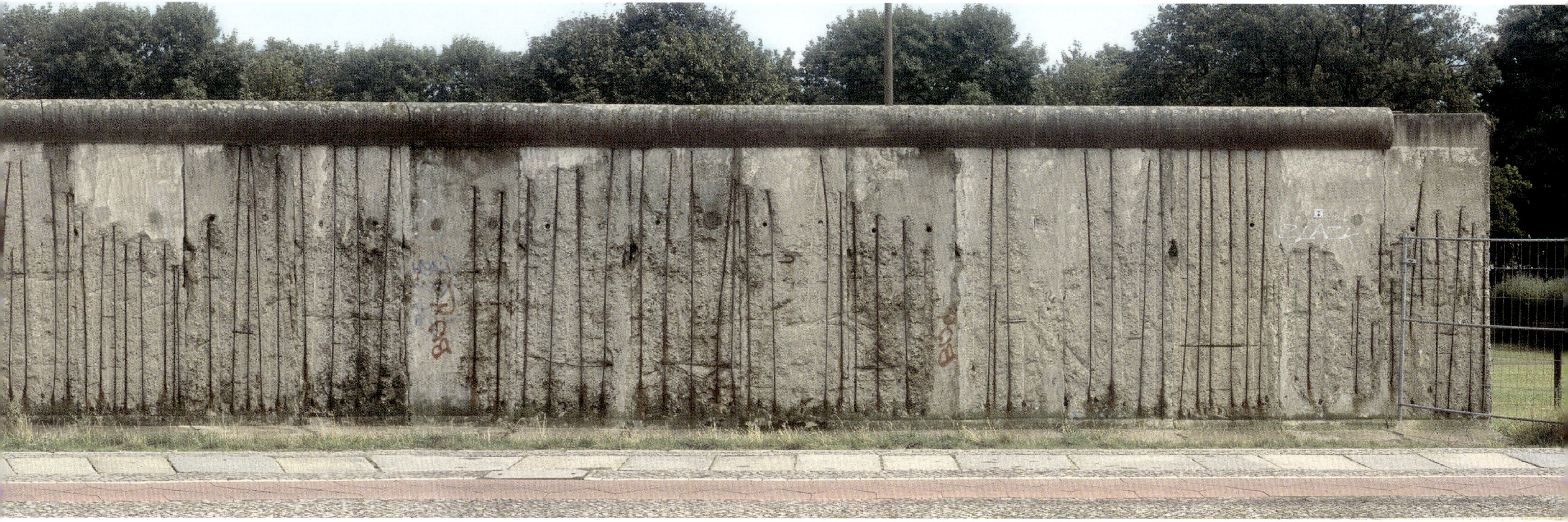

2007 Bernauer Straße →

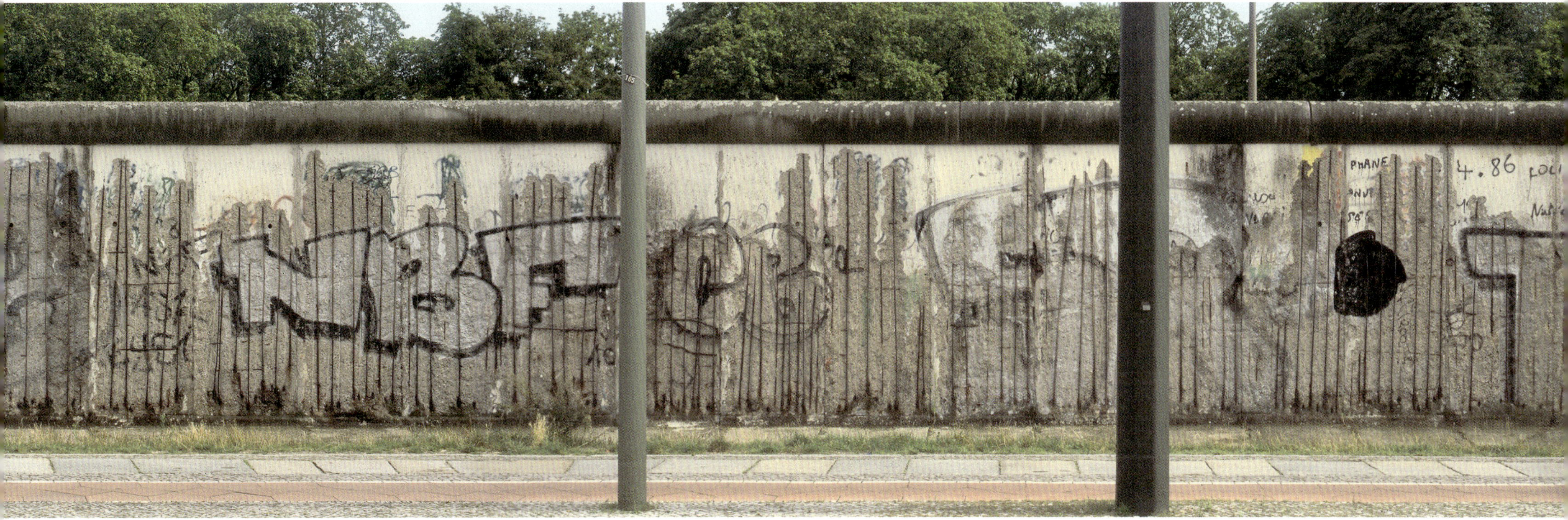
PHANE
4.86

2007 Bernauer Straße →

Funkturm Berlin am Alexanderplatz
The Berlin Radio Tower on Alexanderplatz

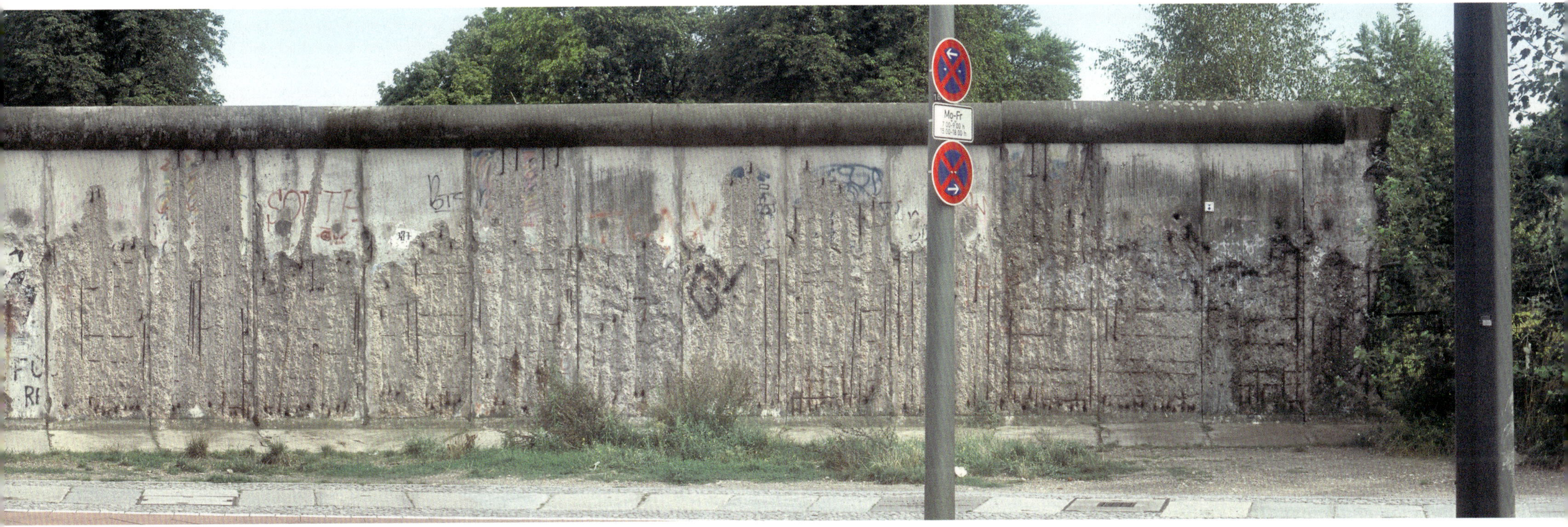
Mo-Fr
7.00-9.00 h
15.00-18.00 h

Die Teilung Berlins
Ausschnitt der Karte Seite 2
Division of Berlin
Detail of the map page 2

F   Französisch besetzte Zone
    French Sector
UDSSR Sowjetisch besetzte Zone
    Sowjet Sector
USA Amerikanisch besetzte Zone
    American Sector
GB Britisch besetzte Zone
    British Sector

— Verlauf der Berliner Mauer
  Course of the Berlin Wall

···· Entlang dieser Strecke
  entstanden die Fotografien
  *The photos were taken along
  this part of the course*

— Besetzte Zonen *Sectors*

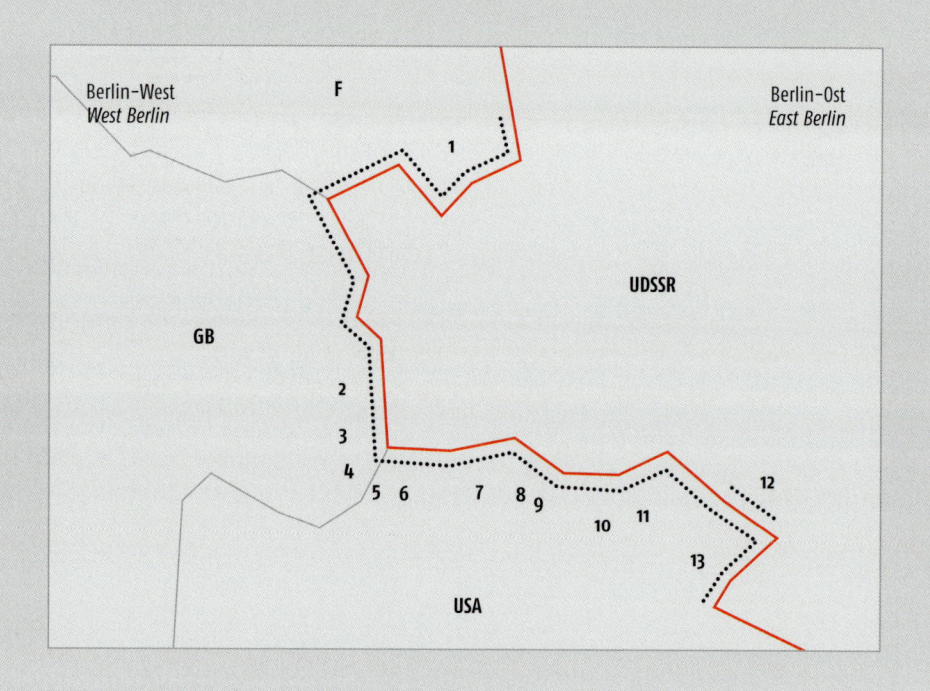

1 Bernauer Straße
2 Ebertstraße
3 Potsdamer Platz
4 Stresemannstraße
5 Niederkirchnerstraße
6 Zimmerstraße
7 Axel-Springer-Straße
8 Sebastianstraße
9 Luckauer Straße
10 Luckauer Straße, Waldemarstraße
11 Bethaniendamm
12 Mühlenstraße (East Side Gallery)
13 Lohmühlenstraße

Index nach Malern
Index by artist

Index nach Straßen
Index by street

54, 55	Christian Benazet	37 – 39	Axel-Springer-Straße
27, 28	Jonathan Borowski	48 – 66	Bethaniendamm
35, 49, 50, 51, 54, 55, 56, 57, 59, 62, 63	Christophe Bouchet	14 – 19	Bernauer Straße (1984 bis 86)
66	Mark Eins	80 – 91	Bernauer Straße (2007)
35	Felix und Vera	19 – 20	Ebertstraße
53, 55, 56	Michael Gremenz	67 – 69	Lohmühlenstraße
52, 53	Alexander Hacke	42 – 47	Luckauer Straße, Waldemarstraße
65	Richard Hambleton	76 – 79	Mühlenstraße (East Side Gallery)
65	Indiano	22 – 33	Niederkirchnerstraße
35, 46, 48, 50, 51, 56, 59, 62	Thierry Noir	70 – 75	Potsdamer Platz
68	Martin von Ostrowski	40 – 41	Sebastianstraße
69	Paul Revellio	20 – 21	Stresemannstraße
54	Jean-Martin Tandetzki	34 – 36	Zimmerstraße
42, 43, 44, 45, 46, 60, 61	Uli		
26, 27, 28, 29	Peter Weiss		
24	Zephyr		

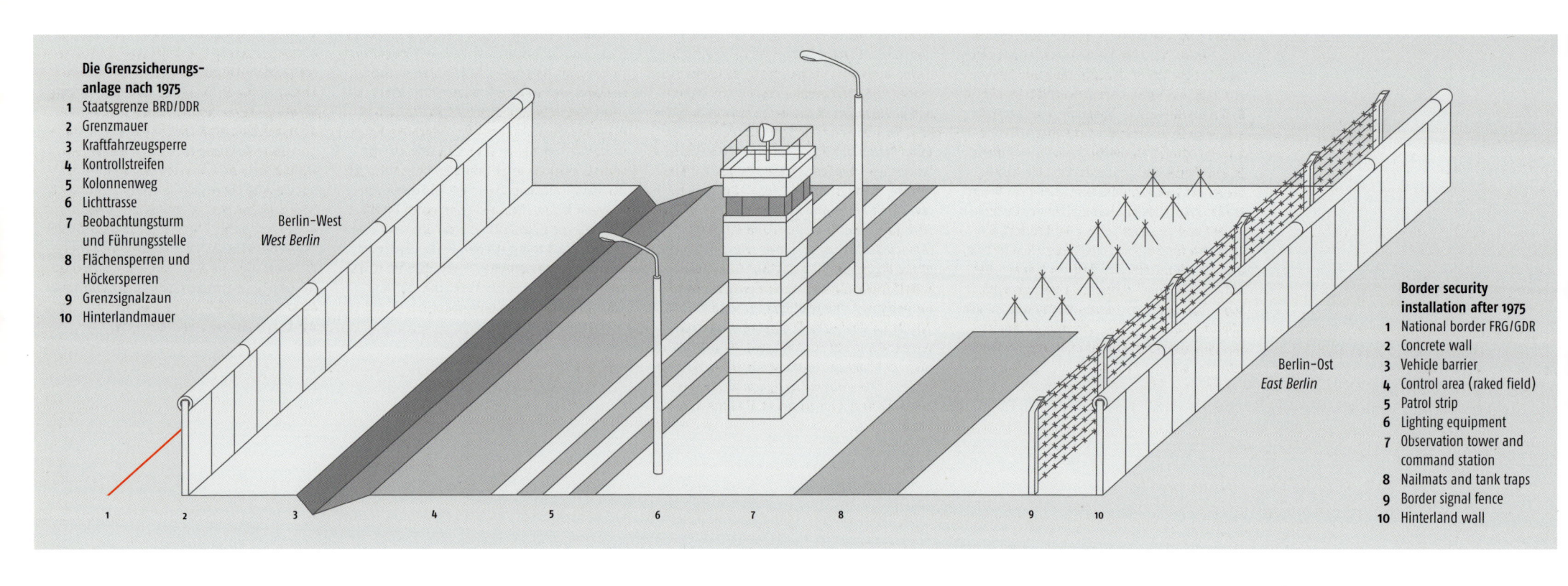

Die Grenzsicherungsanlage nach 1975
1. Staatsgrenze BRD/DDR
2. Grenzmauer
3. Kraftfahrzeugsperre
4. Kontrollstreifen
5. Kolonnenweg
6. Lichttrasse
7. Beobachtungsturm und Führungsstelle
8. Flächensperren und Höckersperren
9. Grenzsignalzaun
10. Hinterlandmauer

Berlin-West
West Berlin

Berlin-Ost
East Berlin

Border security installation after 1975
1. National border FRG/GDR
2. Concrete wall
3. Vehicle barrier
4. Control area (raked field)
5. Patrol strip
6. Lighting equipment
7. Observation tower and command station
8. Nailmats and tank traps
9. Border signal fence
10. Hinterland wall

Biografie
Biography

Armin Lindauer studierte in Düsseldorf, Konstanz und Berlin. Von 1984 bis 2003 war er mit eigenem Design-Atelier in Berlin tätig und lehrte von 1984 bis 1997 an der Universität der Künste Berlin Grafik-Design, Typografie und Fotografie. Seit 2000 ist er Professor für Editorial Design und Typografie an der Hochschule Mannheim. Er veröffentlichte unter anderem „Die Berliner Mauer mit Daten und Fakten", „Rund um Berlin", beides Leporellos mit Fotografien der Berliner Mauer und „Helmut Lortz | Denkzettel", ein Lehrbuch für Gestalter. Die Fotografien in dem vorliegenden Buch „Die Berliner Mauer – Der Anfang vom Ende" entstanden 1984 bis 1986, 1991, 1999 und 2007. Seine Arbeiten wurden mit über dreißig nationalen und internationalen Designpreisen ausgezeichnet. Armin Lindauer lebt und arbeitet in Mannheim und Berlin.

Armin Lindauer studied in Düsseldorf, Constance and Berlin. From 1984 to 2003 he worked in Berlin in his own design studio, and from 1984 to 1997 he taught graphic design, typography and photography at the Berlin University of the Arts. Since 2000 he has been Professor for Editorial Design and Typography at the Mannheim University of Applied Sciences. His publications include, amongst other things, "Die Berliner Mauer mit Daten und Fakten" (The Berlin Wall with facts and figures), "Rund um Berlin" (Around Berlin), both fanfolds with photographs of the Berlin Wall and "Helmut Lortz | Denkzettel" (Helmut Lortz | Reflections), a textbook for designers. The photographs in this book "The Berlin Wall – The Beginning of the End" were taken in 1984 to 1986, 1991, 1999 and 2007. His works have been awarded over thirty national and international design prizes. Armin Lindauer lives and works in Mannheim and Berlin.

Dr. Andreas Schenk, wurde 1961, dem Jahr des Mauerbaus, in Reicheneck (Baden-Württemberg) geboren. An der Universität Tübingen studierte er Kunstgeschichte und promovierte über russischen Kirchenbau. Nach einer Lehrtätigkeit an der Staatlichen Akademie der Bildenden Künste in Stuttgart, in der er das Fach Baugeschichte vertrat, arbeitete er zeitweise im Denkmalschutz der Stadt Mannheim. Seit 1998 ist Schenk vorwiegend freiberuflich tätig und durch Veröffentlichungen und Ausstellungen zur Baugeschichte Mannheims hervorgetreten. Derzeit ist er als Kurator der Ausstellung „Geschichte im Plakat 1945–1963" tätig. Andreas Schenk lebt und arbeitet in Mannheim und Tübingen.

Dr. Andreas Schenk was born in 1961, the year of construction of the Berlin Wall, in Reicheneck (Baden-Württemberg). He studied art history at the University of Tübingen, writing his doctorate on Russian church architecture. After teaching Architecture History at Stuttgart State Academy of Art and Design, he worked for a time in protection of historical buildings of the city of Mannheim. Since 1998, Dr. Schenk has worked mainly as a freelance, making his mark through publications and exhibitions on the architectural history of Mannheim. He is currently employed as the Curator of the exhibition "Geschichte im Plakat 1945–1963". Andreas Schenk lives and works in Mannheim and Tübingen.

Impressum
Imprint

Copyright © 2009
Edition Panorama
armin lindauer | sehwerk

Edition Panorama GmbH
G 7, 14; 68159 Mannheim
Germany
Phone +49 (0) 621 32 88 69 0
Fax +49 (0) 621 32 88 69 20
info@editionpanorama.de
www.editionpanorama.com

ISBN 978-3-89823-404-7

Photographs All rights reserved
Printed in Germany
© Armin Lindauer and
Edition Panorama

No parts of this book may be
reproduced in any form or
by any electronic or mechanical
means without written
permission from the publisher
Edition Panorama, Germany.

Concept, Design, armin lindauer | sehwerk
Photograph Berlin, Mannheim
www.arminlindauer.de
www.sehwerk.org
Typesetting Bianca Radke, Armin Lindauer
Text Andreas Schenk, Armin Lindauer
Translation Global-Text, Heidelberg | Mark Woolfe
Text Armin Lindauer by Natalie Wilcock
Image editing EPS GmbH, Speyer
Bernd Fix, Bernd Grill, Jürgen Imberg
Printing abcdruck GmbH, Heidelberg
Bookbinding Buchbinderei Schaumann GmbH,
Darmstadt
Font FF Fago